Provided
by

Measure B

which was approved by
the voters in
November, 1998

WHEN THE
TUNA
WENT DOWN
TO
TEXAS

WHEN THE TUNA WENT DOWN TO TEXAS

HOW BILL PARCELLS LED THE COWBOYS BACK TO THE PROMISED LAND

MIKE SHROPSHIRE

William Morrow
An Imprint of HarperCollinsPublishers

WHEN THE TUNA WENT DOWN TO TEXAS. Copyright © 2004 by
Mike Shropshire. All rights reserved. Printed in the United States
of America. No part of this book may be used or reproduced in
any manner whatsoever without written permission except in the
case of brief quotations embodied in critical articles and reviews.
For information address HarperCollins Publishers Inc., 10 East
53rd Street, New York, NY 10022.

HarperCollins books may be purchased for educational, business,
or sales promotional use. For information please write: Special
Markets Department, HarperCollins Publishers Inc., 10 East 53rd
Street, New York, NY 10022.

FIRST EDITION

Designed by Jeffrey Pennington

Printed on acid-free paper

Library of Congress Cataloging-in-Publication Data

Shropshire, Mike.
    When the Tuna went down to Texas : how Bill Parcells led
the Cowboys back to the promised land / Mike Shropshire.—
1st ed.
        p.   cm.
    ISBN 0-06-057211-6 (alk. paper)
    1. Dallas Cowboys (Football team)   2. Parcells, Bill.   I.
Title.
GV956.D3S57 2004
796.332'64'097642812—dc22   2004054663

04 05 06 07 08 WBC/RRD 10 9 8 7 6 5 4 3 2 1

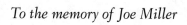

To the memory of Joe Miller

CONTENTS

CONTENTS

FOREWORD

Few individuals in Texas really knew or appreciated who Bill Parcells actually was when Jerry Jones hired him to coach his football team. I didn't.

When Bill Parcells's best teams were up, the Dallas Cowboys' best teams were down. A Bill Parcells–coached team never played against the Cowboys even in a playoff game, much less a Super Bowl. As far as I was concerned, Bill Parcells was just another Rich Kotite who'd managed to get a few lucky bounces.

Parcells was from New Jersey. I didn't know anything about New Jersey, other than that that's where the airliner I happened to be riding on frequently had to circle before it landed at LaGuardia. I asked somebody who'd lived there about the place, and he said, "New Jersey is where all the young men live in neighborhoods or townships where they form gangs and beat the crap out of each other, all of the girls put out on demand, and everybody has an Italian mother who insists they eat three large helpings of spaghetti before they hit the streets, knowing that'll keep the kids from getting too drunk."

So, armed with that insight, I decided to write a short book about Bill Parcells, aka the Tuna, and his impact on his new team, the Cowboys. Quick research on Parcells promptly indicated that all the people back east, the legion that worships the man, regard the Tuna as an enigma. Actually, he's not. Check out

Bill Parcells's birthday: August 22, 1941. That's right on what the astrology nuts call the cusp, splitting the fairway between Leo and Virgo.

The Leo is "unchangeable, despising of flattery, tyrannical, kingly, marketing in pride and strength that often lapse over into megalomania." Well, that's Bill Parcells right down to his toenails, okay? (Here's something else I learned about Parcells: He ends almost every sentence he utters with "okay?" to the extent that anybody who's been around him long enough starts doing that, too.)

As for the Virgo, we learn: "While Leo is concerned with largeness and greatness, Virgo is concerned with details. The Virgo has a distinct sense of what is real and thinks things through before acting."

You'd think, then, that the zodiac solves the riddle of Bill Parcells. So then, how does the regal Leo and the detail-oriented Virgo evolve into a creature who, after driving across the path of a black cat, will put the car in reverse and back up across the path again to remove the curse and, after owning up to such a bizarre fixation, get himself in trouble with animal rights groups that believe the Tuna is obsessed with running over house pets while driving backward?

By watching Bill Parcells and what amounts to a miracle season with the Dallas Cowboys—America's Team—I would learn life's ultimate lesson: The truth is not always stranger than fiction, but it's a hell of a lot funnier.

CHAPTER 1

THE JOCK WHISPERER

Amid the vast and endless sociological sprawl that erupts from the flat and brownish plains of modern North Texas, where the human species exists as a colony of ants—they may be ants that drive colossal SUVs, but ants nevertheless—there's a peculiar sanctuary that lies in sublime isolation from the twenty-first-century suburban madhouse that surrounds it. The homes that line the thoroughfares of this odd place, with their gray rooftops and stucco walls of cream and reddish orange, fronted by tiny yards that contain an allotment of two live oak trees that are really more like big weeds than trees, conform to the universally enforced code of impersonality that is the signature of the Sunbelt residential compound. Here is what separates this place from the numbing norm.

Look at these residential street signs: Cowboys Parkway, Avenue of Champions, Dorsett Drive, Meredith Drive, Staubach Drive, Morton Court. There's a thoroughfare named after almost every Dallas Cowboys icon, living or otherwise. Truax Drive. Billy Truax, for God's sake! They've memorialized a tight end who played maybe two seasons for the Cowboys, and there are more houses on his street than on Landry Lane. George Andrie, one of two Cowboys to score a touchdown in that Ice Bowl game at Green Bay that—even with the cleansing power of the passage of time—won't ever seem to go away, George has got his street. The other player to score that day, Lance Rentzel, has been excluded, but only because residential developers apparently maintain some silly prejudice against convicted flashers.

Pete Gent experienced a mediocrity-shrouded playing career. He is famous for his novel *North Dallas Forty,* in which the hero is a shoe box full of barbiturates, and the Tom Landry character is depicted as the second coming of John Wilkes Booth. God awmighty, even Pete Gent has a street named after him. This is football's version of Neverland, and Texas happens to be one of the very few venues on this planet where such a domain could happen.

Welcome to Valley Ranch, and please do not be deceived by the word "ranch." You won't find any horses or heifers or Gene Autrys or peckerwood rustlers or any of the other stereotypical features that one associates with the concept of a ranch. Situated a few blocks away from the seesaws and slides at Champions Park, not far from the intersection of Winners Avenue and Touchdown Drive, is where you will locate the corporate headquarters of a notorious enterprise. You'll drive past the topiary-hedged star surrounded by the Austin stone facade, and suddenly you're in there, the realm of what the blue-and-white sign identifies as WORLD CHAMPIONS—1971, 1977, 1992, 1993, 1995. The compound is crisp, immaculately combed, tweezed, and manicured, yet characterized by all of the warmth and hospitality of a munitions factory.

This is the home office of the most publicized, most cherished, most feared, and most despised organization in all of sports—the Dallas Cowboys.

And yet, even with all of the palpable otherworldly effects that shroud the complex, it is not a place where one might expect to encounter a zombie, a card-carrying member of the Amalgamated Brotherhood of the Undead, prowling the hallways. I thought that the one outstandingly inexplicable event of my life, my only brush with the supernatural, happened when I saw what was surely the specter of Andrew Jackson. For the merest trace of an instant, accompanied by a loud clap of thunder, Old Hickory appeared beside me on the front veranda of the Hermitage.

The Ghost of Valley Ranch is even more compellingly eerie. Death, I have seen thy face, and thy name is Tuna.

Throughout Western civilization, the one true and enduring cultural reality is that Monday is God's joke on the workingman. Shake off the hangover and commence yet another five to six days' worth of failed dreams and lost ambitions. That's for the lucky ones.

Bill Parcells's Mondays, it is unsettlingly evident, summon a dimension of torment that no reasonable man could fathom—no sweat-soaked peon swinging a machete in the snake-infested sugarcane plantations in Castro's Cuba, no pin-striped Philadelphia barrister with an ulcerated gut from attempting to achieve a junior partnership—nothing that any of these doomed souls could even begin to comprehend. When Parcells decided to reenter the coaching rackets and come to Dallas, his former secretary with the New York Jets placed a call to the woman in the Cowboys office who would be her latest counterpart. She offered some advice. On Mondays, Bill Parcells should be avoided like cholera.

Parcells, the football coach, had spoken of a hidden force that seizes his brain and his body. When the final gun sounds on Bill Parcells's NFL Sunday, the curse begins, and it won't release its gnarled and twisted fingers from the Tuna's throat for thirty-six diabolic hours, at least. He must gather the game tapes, poring over them, reviewing the activities of every player on every play, evaluating, second-guessing, anguishing over this football game so inconsequential to the world as a whole. Eleven players, each seemingly vulnerable to about eleven things he might do wrong. The potential for imperfection then becomes eleven multiplied by eleven. Given football's laws of chaos, a usually trustworthy tight end, with his team facing second and goal, will inexplicably move a half-count early, and the five-yard penalty turns 7 potential points into 3. Those are the kinds of things that the Tuna finds on these tapes, the microscopic subplots that make his cardiovascular arteries constrict and impel him ever closer to the hereafter.

He sits alone in his office. In another part of the building is the locker room that is decorated by Tuna billboards offering such reminders as BLAME NOBODY—EXPECT NOTHING—DO SOMETHING, LOSERS SIT AROUND IN SMALL GROUPS, BITCHING ABOUT THE COACH, THE SYSTEM, AND OTHER PLAYERS, AND WINNERS COME TOGETHER AS A TEAM. It is dark, vacant, and quietly eerie.

Two A.M. Four. The first traces of sunlight appear through the window of his Valley Ranch office. The Tuna craves sleep. He knows it won't happen until he endures his Monday. Parcells spoke of his condition during the heat of the 2003 football season. He called himself "cra—," stopping just short of adding the second damning syllable, the "zy."

But when I saw this haunted shell of a human on that Monday at Valley Ranch, his face the color of month-old ashes in a fireplace, I knew that this man was not "cra—," but the victim of an ancient curse cast upon his being from—well—six thousand years in the past. No, you're not nuts on Monday. You're a freakin' zombie. You can look it up, Bill. A zombie, according to the official handbook of the American Medical Association, is "a soulless body who has been revived by death and can be made to work like a slave."

Let's probe more deeply into this Tuna-zombie syndrome. According to people who know zombies, drink beer, and go bowling with them, they are "beings that behave like us and may resemble our functional organizations and even perhaps our neuro-physiological makeup without conscious experiences or components."

Yep. That's Big Bill.

One of the world's leading authorities on zombies, Jaron Lanier, has written, "Arguing with zombies is generally futile, of course, but there's a lot to be learned from zombies; they are useful, at the very least, as a conversation piece." Any person who has associated with Bill Parcells in any capacity—player, coach, front office, media—would have to agree that Mr. Lanier must have been talking about Bill Parcells.

That's the creature who was on display at Valley Ranch, the one who had been up all through the night watching the videotape of his team's final regular season game, a loss, a wasted afternoon at the Super Dome in New Orleans. His team had played a crappy game. They had lost to the Saints, 13–7. The highlight of the game from the Dallas perspective happened in the third quarter when defensive end Eric Ogbogu had raced onto the field and prepared to line up when somebody noticed that he wasn't wearing a helmet. Throughout his career, Parcells had never seen any player pull a stunt like that.

Now, on a Texas December morning just three days short of the New Year, Parcells sits in a hallway alcove at Valley Ranch and greets a handful of media visitors. He stares at them through fresh-from-the-grave eyes. They're open but express no emotion, no life at all.

"Coach," someone asks gently, "going to any New Year's Eve parties?"

Now the zombie comes to life. "That's this week, right?"

Aha, the creature is alive. It speaks of the demon that inhabits its soul, the one that chased Steve Spurrier—seemingly a Chosen One for NFL coaching success if ever there had been one—away from the Redskins and out of the league after two mere seasons. Spurrier had up and quit in D.C. that very morning. There is a fiendish side to the task of coaching at this level, an all-consuming negative force field that made Tom Landry cry and drove Vince Lombardi to an early death.

"During the day, the men maintain the cloak of bravado in which they wrap their self-respect; at night, alone in the darkness, their grief and fright sometimes become too much to bear." That's a passage from Alfred Hassler's *Diary of a Self-Made Convict*. Rather than describing the plight of men forever confined behind cold granite, Hassler might just as well have been transcribing the world of the pro football coach. During the twilight of his performing career, Harry Houdini used to bitch and moan about the burnout that happens with persons occupying jobs in the public eye. Every time Harry went to work, somebody would lace him into a straitjacket, lock him in a safe, and then throw him off the Brooklyn Bridge. He wanted to quit, but his wife wouldn't hear of it because he was making so damn much money. Houdini had it easy compared with coaching in the NFL.

Paul Brown. Don Shula. Bud Grant. Steely-eyed and jut-jawed, profiles that belong on a silver dollar—boy, did they put on the brave front. In private moments, you can be sure that there were a multitude of occasions when they sat jabbering to themselves like Humphrey Bogart in his unforgettable portrayal of Fred C. Dobbs in *Treasure of the Sierra Madre,* a man impelled into lunacy by gold fever. "To live the life that I have to live, if you don't get results, it's not worth it," Parcells intones.

This is the Monday Bill, remember, the Bill Parcells the world seldom sees. It was amazing to realize that the man in the trance had just completed one of the greatest coaching performances since Morris Buttermaker and the Bad News Bears won the big one. Thanks to the Tuna, the Dallas Cowboys were back in the NFL playoffs.

Cowboys owner Jerry Jones, a man involved in a courageous struggle to overcome what had been diagnosed as a terminal face-lift, had enticed Parcells to leave his self-imposed exile in the ESPN studios and come on down into the land of God, guns, and NASCAR as an act of sheer desperation.

What the Tuna had accomplished was to transform a team that was so sick it had bedsores, and he had transformed it into a winner. The Dallas Cowboys, after becoming the NFL's version of Attila's Huns in the early 1990s, had started to display symptoms of illness in 1996. To the unbridled delight of the vast legions of football fans who have long loathed the silver-star bullies, the decay had metastasized to the point that Dallas had suffered three consecutive 5–11 seasons.

Do not be deceived by the accumulated fifteen wins, though. The fact was that on fifteen occasions, the Cowboys were fortunate enough to encounter some teams that somehow managed to play so beneath themselves that they declined to Dallas's bottom-feeding level. That happens a lot in the NFL. This team didn't need a coach; it needed a faith healer, some radio evangelist who sells autographed pictures of Jesus Christ and heals cripples. But since all of Jerry Jones's dollars were not sufficient to get one of those, he hired Bill Parcells, a man who had been known to have performed some miracles of his own.

The year 2003 was when *Seabiscuit* hit the theaters and earned an Oscar nomination, but the Tuna's almost instantaneous revitalization of the Dallas Cowboys far and away ranked as the Feel-Good story of the year. And upon further review, as they like to say in the NFL, it was found that there are odd parallels that connect the racehorse epic with the Parcells Texas saga.

Let's begin with the owners. Seabiscuit's Charles Howard assembled a fortune in the years just after the turn of the previous century with his natural talents as a huckster. He sold a product for which there was little or no demand at the time—automobiles. After Howard's son died when he went off a cliff in one of those damned automobiles, what did the grief-stricken Howard do? He ditched his wife and married his daughter-in-law's little sister, a Mexican actress. Then Howard began to buy Thoroughbred racehorses, and from this, one thing becomes strikingly evident. Beneath the heroic trappings of the book and the motion picture, Charles Howard was a man driven by an urgent need—to consider himself attractive to younger women.

When it comes to performing the art form known as the Great American Hustler, Jerry Jones would not take a backseat to Charles Howard. From the time Jones was a pup, he lived his life in strictest accord with one ethic: Get rich or die trying. As to the motivation to be appealing to the chicks of his children's generation, Jerry sought a new and magical youthful appearance. Thus the face-lift. In its earliest post-op phase, Jones was described by a Dallas broadcast personality as looking like "Joan Rivers with a pelt on her head."

At the beginning of the *Seabiscuit* tale, remember, the mistrained racehorse, despite regal bloodlines, cannot run in a straight line, overeats, and lies in his stall all day, beating his meat. In this story, instead of a horse, we have a football team. And what a team. Few, if any, organizations in the annals of professional sports can cite more humble beginnings. In the Cowboys' first season, 1960, they actually played an exhibition game against the Los Angeles Rams at the rodeo arena in Pendleton, Oregon. When the officials arrived and inquired where their dressing facilities were located, they were directed to Chute 6. The Cowboys' practice facility that poverty-laced first year was Burnet Field, an abandoned minor-league baseball park located on a floodplain. After practice, all of the uniforms and equipment bags were tied to the rafters so the rats wouldn't eat them.

That's how champions are born, in screenplays at least. The Cowboys, other than during a recession in the 1980s, commenced four unprecedented decades during which time they kicked ass, chased ass, and had the sheer, bald audacity to call themselves America's Team. The rest of America hated that, and the Cowboys' response to the nation was, "If you don't like it, tough shit." No franchise since the inception of the National Football League got good and stayed good longer. The Dallas Cowboys posted twenty consecutive winning seasons, took a breather, then came back and won three more Super Bowls.

By the onset of the new millennium, the Dallas Cowboys had traveled a complete orbit, and as an on-the-field product they were situated at the very rear of the NFL pack. Jerry Jones's team, circa 2002, remained clad in the uniform of a proud champion but were now hopelessly misguided and yet yearning for a wise and steady hand to lead it back to the highway of prosperity.

The individual who would stroke the Biscuit out of his stall and into the winner's circle was the trainer, Tom Smith. Here we had a man whose mind and soul were perfectly molded for the equine kingdom but hopelessly ill-suited for any reasonable interaction with humankind.

Tom Smith, meet your spiritual offspring, Coach Bill Parcells— the Jock Whisperer. Some football coaches may have equaled, but none have yet excelled, the Jock Whisperer's uniquely strange capacity to infiltrate the brains of the individuals who labor beneath his shadow. Some suggest that professional football players exist upon an intellectual plain that lies somewhere between that of the macaw and the polar bear, depending upon what position they play, and that they can actually respond to simple commands.

"Actually, they're just trained pigs," the Jock Whisperer has insisted on at least two occasions since arriving in Texas. Whatever the species, Bill Parcells inspired his menagerie like nothing seen before throughout the 2003 season.

The fourth piece of the *Seabiscuit* package was the jockey, Red Pollard. Poor bastard. A lost soul, existing in the depths of the tank tracks and living inside of stalls. A Shakespeare-reciting, two-fisted jug boxer, he was poised on the doorstep of oblivion until Tom Smith spotted some rare trait, previously undetected, hidden deep in the boy's innards that signaled to the trainer that Red Pollard had the mojo it takes to ride a winner.

Granted, this is a stretch, but in the Tuna's Texas tale, Red Pollard's counterpart is represented in quarterback Quincy Carter. Here's Carter's résumé: failed minor-league baseball player in the Cubs' chain with a lifetime .217 batting average; spotty collegiate career with the Georgia Bulldogs; celebrated as the joke of the 2001 NFL draft after Jones mandated his pick in the second round; banished to the bench, seemingly once and forever, after throwing a couple of hideous interceptions at Arizona. Yet the Tuna—like Tom Smith the trainer had detected a special aura in jockey Red Pollard—scrutinized Carter throughout the various preseason camps and located an elusive, esoteric something in this long-tongued lad who inscribed by hand a Bible verse on the back of his undershirts. Actually, Parcells really didn't see a damn thing that was special about Quincy Carter, other than that he was less incapable than the alternative, Chad Hutchinson. So the Tuna selected Carter to—as Big Bill expressed it—"drive the bus."

For this adventure to ultimately offer the heartwarming potential of the *Seabiscuit* epic, and the way I'd really prefer to end this thing, Quincy Carter would rise from the Cowboys' bench and run ninety-nine yards in a body cast for the winning touchdown in the Super Bowl while women swooned, grown men wept, and Janet Jackson whipped both of 'em out.

Well, it didn't quite happen that way. In our final chapter, the Cowboys go one-and-done in the NFC, getting the crap kicked out of them by the Carolina Panthers.

Still, the spectacle of Bill Parcells squeezing ten wins out of this turkey of a football team is the best damn story many football people in Texas have seen in years. So here it is.

CHAPTER 2

TWO HOOKERS AND THE END OF A DYNASTY

In the next-to-last week of the 2003 National Football League season, Joe Horn, playing for the New Orleans Saints, caught a touchdown pass against the Atlanta Falcons. Horn, exultant in the end zone, produced a cell phone that he'd concealed in his uniform and placed a call.

Thus Joe Horn upstaged San Francisco's Terrell Owens and climbed to the top of the National Football League's competition for post-touchdown audacity. Horn captures the Hot Dog Award. So what if the league fined Horn thirty grand? What an outrage! What a breach of football decorum! What next?

Over in an adjoining state, that being Texas, somebody who did not understand how Bill Parcells runs his factory asked the coach, "If Joe Horn was playing for you and pulled a stunt like that, what would you have done to the guy?"

Parcells, who had concerns of his own, could only shrug. "It wouldn't have happened," he said.

The inquisitor persisted. "Okay. Hypothetically, though. What would . . ."

Again, the Tuna explained that the topic, in this case, was a nontopic. A player on a Bill Parcells football team would sooner take to the field wearing a Peruvian Collection ivory linen slip dress, hand-crocheted in a sweet-pea-vine lace camisole than dance the Waxahachie two-step after registering a sack.

If Bill Parcells has any operational mandates, they are as follows: his players cannot, will not (1) argue with an official, (2) taunt an opponent, (3) celebrate excessively after making a play.

There are subtexts, as well. Individualism on the Parcells ideological chart ranks as a gas chamber offense. On Parcells's New York Jets team, a player such as Keyshawn Johnson—who was born with a lot of Joe Horn in him, as well as a grotesquely enlarged self-image that was deemed incurable—became just another name and number listed upon the fifty-three-player active roster. Keyshawn, after all, was a guy who was contracted to write a book about his pro football experiences before he had played so much as a single down in the NFL. The task of convincing this young man to subvert his natural tendencies toward self-expression and simply play team football is second nature to Parcells. After Johnson played on a Super Bowl champion team at Tampa, he promptly talked himself off the team. Now he is back with Bill Parcells and the Cowboys, and Keyshawn will once again learn to shut up. That's the way it has to be.

Otherwise, a deeper corrosion seeps into the discipline processes of a football organization. That leads to moral decline, and the proudest and best organizations in the league will eventually find themselves in a tailspin. Ernest Hemingway summed up the calamity in *The Sun Also Rises:* "It happens in two ways. Gradually at first, and then all of a sudden." And thus it was with the Dallas Cowboys of the mid-1990s, a great team that lost its moral compass and wound up traveling the path of righteousness on the wrong side of the road.

Pompeii. Troy. Babylon. Angkor. Knossos. The great civilizations of the earth's past follow the same pathways. They rise. They walk hand in hand with the gods. And for reasons of their own, they vanish. So if the Mayan empire was destined to thrive, then disappear without a trace, leaving behind jungle pyramids and sacrificial wells, why, then, should the Dallas Cowboys be expected to endure?

Unarguably, the Cowboys of the early to the mid-1990s will be remembered as the last of the almighty professional football dynasties. The constraints of free agency and salary caps have seen to that. But before mediocrity became the National Football League norm, those Cowboys marched across the competition, as General George Patton used to say, like crap through a goose. This team was a silver-and-blue fortress constructed of equal measures of muscle, hubris, and swagger. The players' mission was not to defeat the foe but to destroy it. Maestros of the Sunday afternoon massacre, those Dallas Cowboys left behind body parts and scorched artificial turf. That was their signature.

Finally, as history always insists, the 'Boys time would come.

But it wasn't a volcanic explosion that triggered their undoing, nor plague, nor asteroids, nor famine. No. In this epoch, the Cowboys' gridiron colossus was placed on the fast track to extinction not by typhoons or invading Mongol hordes but by a couple of precious little hookers.

I was there. I got to see it all.

The time was late June 1996, in Dallas, Texas, and it was hotter than First Baptist hell. The parking lot next to the Lew Sterrett Criminal Courts Building glittered like the blue Pacific at sunrise, as the morning light reflected off the glass containers strewn across the pavement. Thunderbird. Gallo. Italian Swiss Colony. Captain Morgan. Davy Crockett vodka. All of the quality brands were represented here in this parking lot, the threshold to the fifth largest jail in the United States.

This Lew Sterrett Building stands out as one of Dallas's true architectural gems. Here's the best way to take the Dallas tour: drive west through downtown along Elm Street, past the Texas Schoolbook Depository Building, Dealey Plaza, the grassy knoll (a term that first appeared in a certain trilogy by Tolkien), and *voilà*, there it is, the Lew Sterrett Building, a structure dominated by an arching doorway, a massive upside-down U that offers the impression of a frown. As well it should, since the people within truly constitute the central nervous system of the human predicament—a genuine assembly of Lone Star fuck-ups. Locals who are familiar with the place, the guys who speak fluent Texanese, simply call it Sturt, as in, "Lonnie didn't come home for three days. I called the morgue, hoping he might be there, but he wasn't. So I figgered they've got him locked up down at Sturt."

Yeah, Sturt is perpetually jammed with the Lonnies of the world, and the Willies, and the Juans. But occasionally, every so

often, somebody passes through that frowning, scowling doorway who is a not a poor, simple refugee from society's shit heap.
That's when you will see the small armada of TV trucks, with the
big satellite transmission dishes, parked in a long row in front of
the grim red stockade on Industrial Boulevard. When the satellite trucks appear, you can be sure that a personage from the
Dallas Fete Set has screwed up and that the public is going to get
a good show.

In this case, the man on display happened to be a real,
twenty-four-karat icon. The opera can boast all it wants of
Pavarotti, Carreras, and Domingo. Screw them. The Dallas Cow-
boys had three star tenors of their own—Aikman, Smith, and
Irvin—and the prettiest of that ensemble was Michael Irvin, the
Playmaker, All-Pro receiver, and Hall of Fame party boy. A young
woman who once had a bit part on *One Life to Live* had seen
Irvin enter Terrelli's, a Dallas nightclub, and gushed that
"Michael has an aura, I mean, like, he actually seems to glow.
He's—well—he's beautiful." Michael was now staring into the
face of felony drug charges, cocaine possession to be exact, after
some Irving, Texas, cops raided a suite at a Marriott and found
the dope, a superstar, a retired tight end, and two young ladies
who earned their livelihoods dancing and providing other elements of offstage entertainment.

A pretrial hearing was taking place in one of the criminal
courtrooms. The Playmaker was there and so were the two girls,
Angela Beck and Jasmine Nabwangu. Precious, delicate little
mocha princesses, they could, it appeared, stand in the palm of
your hand. They sat just inside the rail looking oh-so-vulnerable
and yet quite serene while I was positioned in the first row of the
courtroom, where the noncombatants get to sit. They were so

17

close, I could have reached over and touched them. It was the biggest thrill I had experienced in thirty-five years as a journalist.

About twelve feet to the girls' left, the Playmaker sat surrounded by his quartet of lawyers, staring straight ahead, pretending that the girls weren't there—pretending that they were invisible. Perhaps Irvin didn't recognize them with their clothes on.

This was a courtroom, after all, not a nightclub, and the Playmaker wasn't glowing now. The lamp was turned off.

The hearing didn't amount to much. Formalities. A trial date was finalized. Everyone got up and left, but three things were clearly established: (1) once the trial began, it would become precedent, not as the proverbial media circus but as sleazy, low-rent, poor-taste courtroom burlesque, (2) Irvin would get the shaft, and (3) the image and reputation of the Dallas Cowboys football franchise was going to experience a deep and extended excursion into the sewer while the nation gaped, with Leno and Letterman leading the jeers.

At the birth of the Texas Republic, when Sam Houston overwhelmed Santa Anna's forces at the Battle of San Jacinto in 1836, a Texas Ranger arrived at the scene the morning after and noted in his journal that dead horses, dead mules, and dead Mexican soldiers were arranged in piles. The Ranger pointed out that while buzzards and coyotes were feasting on the horses and mules, the scavengers shunned the soldiers, perhaps, the Ranger surmised, "because of the peppery condition of their flesh." Well, that's a cultural outlook that has persisted in Lone Star law enforcement ever since, and it would not be unreasonable to suggest that minorities tend to fare poorly in the Texas criminal justice system.

I am not suggesting, though, that the Playmaker didn't have it coming. Two months before, Irvin, in a demonstration of arrogance that Marie Antoinette couldn't have matched on her best day, arrived for a grand jury appearance all queened up like something out of the pages of a 1949 issue of *Redbook*. A local hairstylist complained that the feathered boa didn't really go that well with the Playmaker's South Philly pimp hat. Apparently, the grand jury agreed with the hairdresser and took about one hundred and eighty seconds to indict Irvin, despite any real evidence.

So Michael was going to take a fall; it was only a question of how far. Henry Wade, the former Dallas County district attorney whose name was always preceded in the local public print with the word "legendary," assured me of that. I always used to enjoy calling Henry, and I could get him to talk about how to prosecute celebrities, people like Jack Ruby. In his career, Wade ("I'm the Wade in *Roe v. Wade,* you know," he used to like to say) went twenty-three for twenty-three when he personally prosecuted what he called death cases. "I don't really know the facts of this particular case, but if the prosecution can get a couple of Lutherans on the jury, then Irvin will get a maximum sentence," Wade assured me.

So the hero of Super Bowls XXIX, XXX, and XXXII, the man whose number 88 Cowboys jersey was worn by approximately 17 percent of the population of North Texas, was flirting with the slammer. "He should be happy he's not locked up, at least," a public defender with the remarkable name of King Solomon told me. "That jail food. I wouldn't flush that stuff down my toilet." King Solomon would resign not long after, having correctly selected the numbers of the Pick Six in the Texas lottery.

The trial itself took on certain trappings of the O. J. Simpson extravaganza that had taken place the previous year. African American football star defendant. Exact gender and ethnic makeup of the prosecution and defense teams. The judge, Manny Alvarez, a poor man's Lance Ito, thriving on the media attention. "The only essential difference," said prosecutor Shannon Ross, the Marcia Clark counterpart, "is that in this one, we don't have two dead victims. We don't have any victims at all, in fact."

Not that a detail like that should inhibit the assembled media from portraying this pissant drug possession rap as the most high-profile courtroom event since Leopold and Loeb or the Tennessee Monkey Trial. Most of the media representatives were of the local TV variety, all of them typical of what Tom Wolfe referred to as "lemon tarts" in his *Bonfire of the Vanities*. Also, there was a reporter for ESPN. A blonde, but she was not of the lemon tart persuasion. Seemingly angry and always intense, you could chop wood with her face.

The sports columnists from the Dallas–Fort Worth papers and around the state killed half of the trees in Oregon, pouring out reams of sanctimonious jive that confirmed to the readers that Irvin was a preening jackass. Interestingly, none of these columnists— not one—bothered to appear in the courtroom to see what might actually be taking place. If they had, they would have seen at once what a farce the proceeding was. When the jury was impaneled, it appeared that somebody was casting a remake of *The Grapes of Wrath*. Twelve solid citizens on leave from the trailer camp. A jury of Michael Irvin's peers? Hardly.

Males in the media were scarce. There was a guy from the Newark *Star-Ledger* and a tall man from *Sports Illustrated* who was relentlessly eager to let everybody know it. And me. A print media sports reporter covering a criminal trial for a local sports talk-show station. That station's entire listenership consisted of gravel haulers whose blood alcohol content hovered around 2.8 by 11:00 A.M. That made my job easier. When one of Irvin's lawyers accused the Irving cops of gestapo tactics, I could simply go on the air, repeat his comments, and say, "This then begs the question: Is this Irving or is this Berlin?" Nobody got it, of course, and my radio career would end when the trial did.

Irvin, at least, had upgraded his look since the ill-starred grand jury appearance, wearing beautifully cut suits, with shirts of light blue or pale yellow that Irvin favors because he likes the way those colors flatter his immaculate mahogany skin. After the morning and afternoon sessions, Irvin, accompanied by his lawyers, walked the length of the hallway to the elevator, staring straight ahead and avoiding the autograph seekers. Two little boys with pens and photos of the Playmaker appeared crestfallen as Michael ignored them and disappeared as the elevator doors slid shut. "Hey, kids!" an ESPN cameraman yelled out. "Michael's two whores are down on the next floor. I bet they'll sign your pictures."

One afternoon, Troy Aikman, the sacredest of all the cows to hit the Dallas athletic scene since Roger Staubach was walking on water, came to the courtroom. The plan was that the jury might deem this as a show of support for a teammate in trouble, of course. But nobody had warned Aikman about these genuinely odd specimens who sat in the jury box. Jojo the Human Anchovy, Bonnie the Blimp, Ronnie the four-legged man—all straight from the midway of the State Fair of Texas. Poor Aikman. He wore the ill-at-ease, embarrassed look of a guy who had just accidentally stumbled into the women's restroom at the bus station.

After a week of predictable testimony by the Irving police who staged the raid, and the desk clerk and the night manager from the Marriott, the show finally became real. The state's star witness—another topless performer named Rachelle Smith, who was not actually on the scene of the bust, but was apparently on intimate terms with persons who were—was about to take the stand.

Smith's boyfriend, a Dallas cop, had just been arrested and charged with conspiring to murder Michael Irvin. Of course, that was no reason for Judge Alvarez to consider a mistrial. Hell no. This was prime-time entertainment, and the judge was getting his fifteen minutes' worth and then some.

Rachelle, a white chick with sandy hair and a sort of countrified mousy look, took the stand. She was fabulous. Under the questioning of prosecutor Mike Gillette, a man whose duplicitous propensities radiated like the heat shimmering off a Texas two-lane blacktop on an August day, Smith told the court about being actively involved at other social occasions that involved Michael Irvin. She talked about drugs. She talked about sex toys. She talked about muff diving with other little dancers while the Playmaker savored his role as a spectator. One of the star players from the Tom Landry Cowboys era, legend has it, would hire prostitutes to visit his own home, then compensate the girls extra to share their love with his male Doberman. But such activities as that were never brought into discussion in the public court, not like this Irvin mess. The expression on the faces of those chalk eaters on the jury was priceless, something I will savor for a lifetime. The highlight of the presentation came when Smith described how Michael forced her into a closet and conducted a personal search of her body cavities, looking for hidden microphones planted by the DA's office.

"And then," she told the court, "Michael said, 'You must never tell Mike Gillette the truth about the drugs, because he is a brave and powerful man, and I fear him.' And I said, 'But Michael, I cannot do that because that would be prejury [*sic*].'"

Mike Gillette is a short guy with eyes like little bitty marbles. He could stand on Judge Alvarez's shoulders and come up to Michael Irvin's belly button. It seemed apparent that Gillette, if he wanted it, could make a big future for himself in Hollywood. Yeah, his dialogue needed some polish, but nobody could question his plot and his characters.

The reporter from the Newark paper, who had spent his entire expense account in one night while researching the Dallas topless scene, looked at me after Smith's testimony and said, "In the long run, it's the T 'n' A evidence that'll nail him." He talked about interviewing a guy who lived next door to the infamous White House, a minimansion near the Cowboys practice field that Irvin and other high-profile players had leased for purposes of the all-night orgy—a place that Irvin described as "the right place to do the wrong thing."

"The next-door-neighbor guy said that it got so loud one night that he went to the White House and rang the doorbell," the reporter said. "The neighbor said somebody inside asked him who he was and what he wanted, and the neighbor said, 'You got three choices. Either you turn down the music, I call the cops, or you let me come inside and join the party.' After a couple of minutes, the door opened slightly and a huge hand presented him a half gallon of Crown Royal."

Bottle in hand, the neighbor went back home.

After a weekend recess, the trial would continue the following Monday. Prior to Rachelle's much-anticipated retaking of the stand, I chatted with a bailiff, a woman of about sixty, with big hair and a big .38 strapped to her right hip. Evidence from the night of the bust was resting on the prosecution's table in a brown grocery bag from Food Lion.

"You know what's in that bag?" I asked the old hide. "It's a vibrator that operates by remote control."

"Ah, hell," responded the bouffant bailiff. "There's nothing new about that. Those things have been around since the Civil War."

Then—all too soon—the trial was over. The two sides agreed to a plea bargain. Irvin would accept two years' probation. The local Neds at my radio station were livid. "Why in the hell would the DA agree with that plea bargain and let him off? They had him nailed to the cross!" Dallas, in case anyone hasn't heard, happens to be a bastion of compassionate conservatism, and everybody wanted to see the cocky black dude swing. I was broadcasting on a cell phone in a crowded courthouse and talking live to all the pilled-up short haulers. "Damn if I know why they let him walk," I said, and then ripped off the Newark guy's great line about the T 'n' A evidence.

The truth is that the prosecution sought the plea, not the other way around, as most folks assumed. The DA's people knew that upon cross-examination, some conspicuous whoppers from Smith's previous testimony would be revealed. Also, because every other cop on the entire police force had made it with the state's star witness, everybody thought it would be in the best interest of public decorum to pack up and go home.

The aftermath of the lurid courtroom exhibition was bittersweet for most of the participants—but more bitter than sweet for most.

Rachelle Smith got a big payday to pose in *Playboy*. Her

ex-boyfriend, the cop who took the fall in the hit scheme on Irvin, got out of jail after a couple of years and was one of three ex-cons who showed up at a book signing I had to promote a golf novel.

The lawyers, mostly, fared poorly. Irvin stiffed his defense team and would later win $1 million in a libel settlement against the local NBC affiliate for its coverage of a bogus claim by yet another topless dancer that he and tackle Erik Williams had raped her. The Playmaker's football career never really amounted to a damn thing after the trial, though. The jurors, I guess, are all now living in caves.

As for the entity that was really on trial, the Dallas Cowboys had been found guilty in the public eye of all of the seven original sins. Well, six, at least, since the jury was still out on the issue of sloth.

Jerry Kramer, the right guard of the Green Bay Packers who jumped the count and laid the block that put Bart Starr into the end zone in the Ice Bowl, summed up the situation: "Whenever I see the Cowboys on TV, I don't know who to root for—the defense or the prosecution. No, this will never be America's Team. If it is, then woe for America."

After that trial, the Cowboys would slide into seven years of darkness. Oh, they had a moment or two in the 1996 season. They pretty much ended Steve Young's career in a regular season win at San Francisco. Beat the hell out of him, in fact. San Francisco sports columnist Scott Ostler wrote that Young "was like china in a bull closet."

And yet, because of those aforementioned twin mocha princesses, the last of the NFL dynasties was sliced and diced, cooked and done. As the courtroom emptied at last from a drama that might have been a creation of Larry Flynt Enterprises, it was all too apparent that these Cowboys were riding on a freight train to hell. Eventually, the coroner would cite complications from moral decay and lack of leadership and direction as the cause of the demise.

Meanwhile, the surprise team of the 1996 season was preparing for training camp. Bill Parcells, a coach who gravitates to the Super Bowl the same way football players like to do brunch at the All Nekkid XXX Gentlemen's Club, had something special with the New England Patriots.

CHAPTER 3

THAT "BANJO PICKER IN *DELIVERANCE*": THE JERRY JONES STORY

The territory presently known as Arkansas first appears in the archives of civilization in 1541.

History's first notation from what would become known as the Land of Opportunity is written in the memoirs of a Spaniard. He was involved in the expedition led by Coronado, venturing into the New World, looking for gems, precious metals, and chorus girls. According to the memoir, the conquistadors, who were packing heat, marched into a Wichita Indian village on the banks of the Arkansas River. The leader of the pack realized that the Native Americans didn't understand a word of Spanish, so he addressed them in Latin.

This was his proposition: Either announce your submission to your new Father, the Spanish king Ferdinand, and accept Jesus

Christ into your hearts as your Lord and Savior, or we will kill you. You've got five minutes to decide.

The memoir noted that the Wichita Indians looked bewildered at first, and then perplexed as the slaughter ensued.

Nothing much, historywise, would come out of Arkansas for another two hundred years or so. But thanks to the Spanish, a heritage of deplorable karma was etched firmly into the landscape. Thus the adage, "You know what you call a little girl who runs away from home in Arkansas?" A virgin.

In the years before and after the Civil War, as the great American migration to the West was in full flower, another legion of fortune seekers, mostly of the Anglo persuasion this time, would pour through Arkansas. The more ambitious were seeking gold in California, while others simply sought free land and a laid-back lifestyle in Texas. Then there were those with darker motives, men with an innate knack for leverage and exploitation. Realizing the vastness of the riches that were available through vice, they set up camp in Arkansas.

Hell, even pioneers wearing coonskin caps like to party every now and then, and the original white settlers of Arkansas—the Founding Fathers, so to speak—established a backwater Las Vegas.

Looking for booze? Opium? Fill your tank in Arkansas—you won't find any more for three thousand miles. Hookers? Oh, man. Look at these girls. Part Choctaw, part black, part Irish, part Cajun. Talk about mixed-breed exotic.

The growth industry that thrived most was gaming. Cards, of course, and every known form of wagering on contests such as prizefights, horse races, rooster fights—proposition wagers of every conceivable invention—trace their roots to the great state of Arkansas. The refined artistry inherent in the natural gamblers, the cons and the true grifters, became a birthright in Arkansas. That ability to function and prosper in the gray area that lies between the letter of the law and the jailhouse is deeply embedded in the DNA of the Arkansas native.

Look at this cast of all-stars . . . all products of the Razorback State. Amarillo Slim, the Hercules of poker players, the grand champion, was not from Amarillo. Not at first, anyway. Hell, no. Amarillo Slim was born on New Year's Eve, 1928, in Johnson, Arkansas. Titanic Thompson, unquestionably the greatest hustler of all time, came out of Arkansas, well equipped with a repertoire of treacheries that a person can actually absorb from the soil of the foothills of the Ozarks. So did H. L. Hunt, the oil billionaire. His occupation when he migrated to Texas was professional cardplayer. Oil came later. Old man Hunt was illiterate, perhaps subnormal in many intellectual functions, but he was endowed with that special blessed something that is second nature to the children of the Hormel Provinces.

Let's talk about Dizzy Dean. During his prime years as the colorful voice of baseball's game of the week and goodwill ambassador for Falstaff beer, Dean would visit rural golf clubs and lose money, on purpose, to the local yahoos on the course. Then, after the golfing, the card playing would begin, and Old Diz, working in concert with a partner who was maestro of the rigged deck, would rewin his golf losses and treble that sum.

Don't think that Hillary Rodham didn't learn a trick or two during her tenure in Little Rock. As First Lady of the United States of America, Mrs. Clinton used to clean house by gathering groups of thirty and then betting that two of them would have the same birthday.

Which brings us around to Jerry Jones.

Jonesie, whose cheekbones suggest a drop or two of Cherokee blood, insinuated himself into the Dallas scene at a heralded press conference in the early months of 1989. Jones was so full of all things Arkansas, he was about to explode. The grin, the drawl, the hog farm charm, the penchant for saying just the wrong thing. Jerry had it all, and it was plainly on display for the world to see when he stood before God and the assembled media to proclaim that he, Jerry, was the new owner of the Dallas Cowboys, and his old buddy from back in Fayetteville, Jimmy Johnson, was the new coach, while Tom Landry was being fitted for mothballs. And when Jerry told the press that he was going to run the entire operation, the whole show . . . "from jocks to socks" . . . he was not kidding.

The purchase of the Cowboys coincided with the sale of another area franchise, the Texas Rangers baseball team, to a consortium that featured George W. Bush as its operational figurehead.

After Jerry Jones's introductory press-box conference, a Dallas sports columnist pondered the contrasting styles of the two new sports ownerships. "The father of one of the owners is the President of the United States," the guy wrote. "The father of the owner of the other team removed and adjusted his false teeth during his son's first press conference."

In reality, Jerry Jones was not too dramatic an alteration from the previous owner in terms of couth. Bum Bright, a Dallas banker, had bought the franchise from its founder, petro-bucks all-star Clint Murchison, who, according to the book *Double Cross,* was a "business associate" of Sam Giancana.

When the price of a barrel of oil cratered from $40 to $15,

the Texas banks collapsed as well. Bum Bright was strapped and needed to sell the Cowboys. Negotiations took place with Marvin Davis, a Denver got-rocks, to take the team off Bright's troubled hands after the conclusion of the Cowboys' 3–13 season in 1988. During the course of his presentation, Bright entertained Davis with some down-home Texas good ol' boy stories, delivered with that unrestrained Lone Star panache that separates the Texas rich from the Minnesota rich. Bright would later confide to friends that he'd cheerfully mentioned something that he probably otherwise wouldn't have had he known that Davis was Jewish. Eventually, the two never agreed on terms. Bright's son and current business associate, Clay, says he can't confirm the story, but remembers Davis as "this blue-eyed guy" who said his family "made all its money selling gabardine."

Out with Marvin Davis, in with Jerry Jones. Think about it. If Bright and Davis hadn't parted ways, the American sporting public might never have gotten to meet Jerry Jones, the NFL would never have had the thrill of suing him for $33 million for cutting his own licensing deal with Pepsi and Nike, Tom Landry might well have coached the team until the day he died, and the Cowboys franchise, in some context, might have been regarded as perhaps normal.

Clearly, Jerry Jones had rough edges; he was the kind of fellow who would team up with his Arkansas pals for annual rafting and fishing expeditions on the White River that they called the Buttfuckalo. So it wasn't really Jerry's fault that he came across, as one Philadelphia scribe sublimely observed, "like the banjo picker in *Deliverance*."

In fairness to Jones, you can't expect a man from a region where people wear red plastic hog hats to football games (many would smuggle in little baggies of marijuana concealed inside the snouts) to suddenly transform into David Niven.

So if the Cowboys fan base was wondering, "Who in the hell is this guy?" try to imagine what questions and concerns might be running through the minds of the people who were employed by the Dallas Cowboys. They would find out very shortly.

On the Monday following that infamous press conference, Jones assembled the Valley Ranch front-office staff—the PR and marketing people, the workers in the ticket office, the bookkeepers, the receptionists, the people who had been put in place by Tex Schramm, not a few of whom had been with the team since its maiden voyage in 1960.

"I am going to need your help, each and all of you," Jerry told the front-office personnel in an urgent, country-fried Arkansas voice that sounded like Jed Clampitt on helium. "You folks know this business, and I don't, and if this thing is going to continue to work and survive, you're going to have to share your knowledge with me, and at the same time, I am asking for 110 percent of what you have in you. I'm demanding that you give me everything that you've got."

On Tuesday morning, the front-office people stuffed 110 percent of whatever expertise that they owned into their lunch and went back to work at Valley Ranch. And on their desks, they found a memo from Jerry Jones: YOU'RE FIRED.

Those early days of the Jones regime were as chaotic as things can get. By the time I met Jerry Jones for purposes of writing a magazine profile, he was still embroiled in a controversy over some sexist comments he'd made regarding the Dallas Cowboys cheerleaders, a minor scandal that became known as Jigglegate. This, after talking about how great Troy Aikman looked in the shower.

The day I went out to interview Jerry, he was giving a guided tour of the Valley Ranch complex to some visiting oil execs from Western Canada. "This is the Taj Mahal of sportdom!" he was telling the Canucks. "Hell, we spend twenty thousand dollars a month taking care of the lawn."

"The laundry?" asked one of the bewildered Canadians, who evidently were experiencing difficulty comprehending the English that Jerry Jones was speaking.

"No, no," Jerry said, clarifying his previous statement. "You know. The lawn. The grass and trees and all that shit."

Finally the Canadians, stockpiled with a full supply of strange stories that they would tell their more sedate friends back in Calgary, cleared out, and I had Jerry Jones to myself for about an hour. We sat in Tex Schramm's old office. Jones hadn't fired Tex. He didn't need to. After witnessing Jones's performance at that first press conference, Tex couldn't get the hell out of there quickly enough.

The office was practically vacant, not yet adorned with any of Jerry's personal touches. Just two chairs and a desk, upon which sat two silver footballs, the Lombardi Trophy that goes to the Super Bowl champion. Tex hadn't owned those and left them behind.

Jones and I had a mutual friend, a Dallas bond broker and proud Razorback who also had a rock 'n' roll band that he called Daddy Jack and the Seven Screaming Negros. He'd offered me some good background. Daddy Jack had been a regular on those Butt-fuckalo trips. I started the interview by talking about Jerry's family—I was curious about his wife, since someone told me that back in Arkansas, "her father owns a whole county."

"Well, her name's Gene," said Jerry. "She spells it like a

boy—*G-e-n-e*. She made a free throw that won her team the state girls' basketball championship. And later she represented Arkansas in the Miss USA Pageant." I wondered if shooting free throws was Gene's act in the talent competition of the pageant but didn't ask. "And my daughter Charlotte," Jerry went on, "she just graduated from Arkansas and is going to Washington. She got a job on the staff of our congressman, Tommy Robinson, and boy, don't think half the town of Washington, D.C., won't be hitting on Charlotte." Then Jerry grinned that trademark grin of his. I liked Jerry.

We talked about football. "The guy on this team I really like is Nate Newton. He's going to be an All-Pro. Tex Schramm wanted to run him off—said he was nothing but a big, fat slob."

Owning his football team, and the spotlight that came with it, for a man deeply engendered in the ethos of "get rich or die try-ing," this was like reaching the pinnacle of Mount Everest before any asshole with twenty grand could be led handheld up to the top. The Dallas Cowboys. To an Arkansas boy, this had to be the rarest of rarefied air.

Then Jerry made a remarkable comment. "It was a tough thing, firing Tom Landry as the first thing I'd have to do on this job, but my God! Owner of the Dallas Cowboys. This might sound bad, but I kind of think I know what Lyndon Johnson felt like the day Kennedy got shot."

At the conclusion of the talk, Jerry said that the financial risk and the inherent stress that come with owning something as high marquee as the Cowboys were not his greatest concerns. His greatest fear, he said, was the prospect that he might someday get hauled in for drunk driving.

After my magazine piece appeared, I would learn that Jerry wasn't too thrilled with the tone. Our friend Daddy Jack told me that Jones had said, "Jack, go punch that son of a bitch in the jaw. Punch him twice. Once for you and once for me."

Three Super Bowl championships later, I encountered Jerry again. He was seated in a booth of a well-patronized Dallas restaurant and bar known as the Stoneleigh P. He was accompanied by a dark-haired lady of about twenty-three who looked like Snow White, except that she was wearing a sleeveless blouse with her black bra straps dangling over her arms. The woman had unbuttoned the front of Jerry's shirt, and she was dipping her right index finger into a glass of red wine and making little figure-eight designs on Jones's chest. It was one week before the start of the Dallas Cowboys' 1997 training camp, and owner and general manager Jerry Jones did not appear to have his mind focused entirely on football.

When Jones got up to leave, I followed him outside and reintroduced myself.

"Wrote that magazine story about you a few years ago. Heard you didn't like it very much," I said.

"Aw, hell," Jerry said. "That's just water under the goddamn dam. Water under the fuckin' dam."

That reaffirmed my first impression of Jerry Jones. I liked the man.

His jealous detractors all claimed that Jerry's eventual aim was to coach the Cowboys himself. Those accusations were a total and absolute crock. See, Jerry knew from the beginning that in order to coach in the NFL, the first and most mandatory qualification was that the coach have knots in his calves the size of golf balls. Hell, Jerry had legs that were cuter than most of the ones you see on the Cowboys cheerleaders. So, shit, he knew he'd never coach.

All sorts of stories float around about Jones. He's the sort of person people like to talk about. Like the time he was at the Super Bowl in New Orleans and at 6:00 A.M. was seen hammering the French Quarter hot spots, not in a limo but in the backseat of a police car that he'd chartered as a party ride.

Jones, on many occasions, was twisting C-notes into tight little rings, like wedding bands, and giving them away to random young ladies at various self-congratulatory high-society glitter events—just an Arkansas boy's gesture to let them know just how much he appreciated how fucking pretty they were.

But—if not a Cowboys fan, then certainly a member of their local captive audience—I wasn't at all interested in Jerry's nocturnal adventures.

What concerned me, not to mention the majority of Dallas Cowboys fans who eagerly awaited America's Team's return to greatness during the Barry Switzer–Chan Gailey–Dave Campo Depression Era, was not the company that Jerry Jones had been keeping during his private, nightlife hours.

Rather, it was the presence of a person who always seemed to be sitting at Jones's right elbow in his luxury suite at Texas Stadium on NFL Sundays. The man was identified as His Royal Highness Prince Bandar bin Abdulaziz, ambassador to the United States from the Kingdom of Saudi Arabia. This Bandar fellow was married to Princess Haifa Bin Faisal, but you never saw her around. Not in Jones's suite, anyway. Given the Arabs' reputation for the treatment of the female spouse, Bandar probably had her stuck somewhere out there in section 219, in the depths of the south end zone, where all of the Cajuns and drunk Okies get to sit.

At first, I presumed Bandar was simply an imposter. Dallas is crawling with those. Hell, back in the early 1980s, some swarthy, big-nosed dude posing as an oil sheik staged his own dance contest at a Dallas disco and wrote the winners checks for about a half million. The checks turned out to be as worthless as the scumbag who signed them, but it made for good copy in the metro section for a couple of days. So there was no reason not to suspect that Jones, the Arkansas rube, had been sucked in by yet another scam artist.

But no, it turned out that Bandar was exactly the person he claimed to be, appointed ambassador by King Faud bin Abdulaziz Al-Saud, the Custodian of the Two Holy Mosques himself. Later on, the same guy turned up at George W. Bush's ranch down in Crawford, Texas, so Bandar obviously had some clout and was clearly the type of fellow who Jerry Jones would wish to partner up with in some of his drilling ventures.

Along about the time Bandar started showing up at Cowboys home games, circa 1998, I wrote a cover piece for *Inside Sports* magazine under the heading "The Dallas Cowboys Have Fallen and Can't Get Up." It was those kinds of suggestions that used to give Cowboys fans upset stomachs. The magazine received a letter that they eagerly forwarded to me, postmarked Brooklyn and written on three-by-five note cards, scrawled vertically across the horizontal lines on the cards. From the parts of the writing that were legible, the guy claimed to own "special powers" and took credit for drowning Natalie Wood and blowing up the space shuttle *Challenger,* and then pointed out that if I didn't quit saying unflattering things about the Cowboys, he'd take care of me in some similar fashion.

The temptation was to send that directive along to Jerry Jones. I didn't, of course, but the message that hit home to me was this: Dammit, Jerry, you're supposed to be president and general manager and, as the Arabs might say, Custodian of the Jocks and Socks of the greatest football franchise on these American shores. So quit cozying up to the Prince Bandars of the world and pay more attention to your Valley Ranch day job, Jonesie, because your team is really starting to suck.

CHAPTER 4

THE PETER PRINCIPLE MEETS MURPHY'S LAW: THE DAVE CAMPO STORY

*L*ife, for all it's cracked up to be, plays some ghastly tricks on those who are preordained to have to live it. Take Bill Parcells, a consummate professional and teacher of men, who somehow got the nickname Tuna pinned to his forehead. It happened in the passage of a mere instant, circa 1980, when Parcells was a coaching assistant with the New England Patriots. A player, or group of players, had come to Parcells with some ridiculous proposition, and the coach had responded, "Who do you think I am? Charlie the Tuna?" Thus, the goofy nickname that would hound this proud man for the rest of his days. Parcells could only be thankful that his retort was not, "What kind of Fuckhead do you take me for?"

From there, the so-called Tuna would advance himself to the

zenith of the coaching ranks and establish himself as a dead cinch for eventual enshrinement into the NFL Hall of Fame in Canton, Ohio. Sadly, destiny—fueled by the all-too-human components of burnout, aging, and the fatigue that makes cowards of us all, as Vince Lombardi used to insist—conspired to bring Parcells to a place he would rather not be.

Reality check, soul search, reinvention of oneself—and the rest of the all-you-can-eat agenda of catchphrases that reinforce the artificial hype that a person will embrace after the engine of life has dropped a couple of cylinders down into the oil pan—Bill Parcells must have been toying with these at the outset of the 2002 version of the National Football League season.

Despite all of the psychological defenses the man could muster, there was to be no avoiding the one indisputable truth that enveloped the ex–football coach who watched while the ink dried on his divorce papers. In Bill Parcells's mind, nearly four decades of coaching and a coinciding number of years of marriage were now wispy images of a rapidly vanishing past. His existence had been transformed from Xs and Os to owin' an ex.

Worse than that, Parcells at ESPN was feeling forever relegated from his appointed role as supreme battlefield leader and strategist to that of the "analyst" or "commentator" in the cramped studios of ESPN. Big Bill was one of "them" now, the media, the guys with butts wider than their shoulders, sporting wardrobes that wouldn't pass the dining room dress code at the Ashtabula Salvation Army on Thanksgiving.

Oh, the degradation. While the ESPN assignment might hold certain trappings of dignity in the public eye, Parcells had plunged into the depths of radio, somehow attempting to stand straight and face the mirror, all the while realizing the shameless nature of the first-person promo that was being distributed that went: "I am very excited to be back with *Sporting News Radio*. Last year, I felt we created a great foundation to build a compelling football show on radio. This is a perfect platform for me to express my opinion and analysis each week along with my partners, Will McDonough and Bruce Murray." It's that kind of crap that shadows a great man for a lifetime. Parcells must have known that. A radio career is something for guys who are addicted to NicoDerm and being treated for gout.

So the mighty Tuna gazed into the new NFL season, realizing that all of the excitement, the intrigues and challenges that used to enable him to experience every minute of every day at full throttle (all the while forgetting the termites that were chewing his guts away), all of that now belonged to the Jon Grudens of the world. Gruden, with that cocky smirk that would make George W. Bush appear modest, was down in Tampa about to win a Super Bowl. And if not Gruden, then Bill Callahan at Oakland or perhaps Andy Reid at Philadelphia, a couple of coaches who couldn't carry Bill Parcells's clipboard, all the glory theirs to experience. Bill Parcells? He was an analyst now, professor emeritus of the National Football League, about a half block away from the dustbin.

Oh, well. At least Parcells could look at Coach Dave Campo down in Dallas and find solace. What a sorry-ass circus that was going to be.

S uch a pleasant soiree. I was standing on the balcony of the Café de Paris in Monte Carlo overlooking the storied casino and heartbreakingly blue Mediterranean beyond that. The September evening breeze soothed the soul and enabled the old man to feel perhaps a little less old. Everywhere one looked, Barbie dolls were arm in arm with Ken Lay dolls.

Prince Albert Alexandre Louis Pierre Grimaldi himself—the Marquis of Baux, Grand Officer of the Lion of Senegal National Order, Knight of the Maltese Order, honorary citizen of Carl's Corner, Texas, and regarded in some circles as the most desirable bachelor on the world scene—was telling me how much he really had wanted to make it with Princess Diana. "I was seated next to Diana in the royal box at Wimbledon," Albert recalled, relishing the experience. "There's a photograph of us there. Diana's watching tennis. And I am watching her."

This was in 2002, and I was inhaling the rejuvenating vistas of the Côte d' Azur, completing an assignment for *Sports Illustrated.* It was a profile of the sporting prince, and I was explaining to His Highness about the *SI* jinx and how he sure as hell never wanted to wind up on the cover. "Your plane will crash . . . you'll ski off the side of a cliff . . . something like that," I said. "Best-case scenario, you'll come down with something like, uh, prostate cancer." A member of the Swiss Olympic cycling team, who happened to be married to Paul Anka's daughter, seemed amused by the prince's angst.

And I was thinking, God awmighty, these are my kind of people, and boy, does this beat the crap out of my most notable previous professional incarnation as a newspaper sportswriter covering the Rangers baseball team, sitting in dives like the Blue Ox in Minneapolis listening to some third-string catcher talk about how he was demanding a trade because he didn't like the drug laws in Texas.

But the morning would come, and reality with it, and I was in the Air France lounge in Nice, sipping a sassy Chardonnay and pondering my return to the Lone Star State, where the tattoos outnumbered the teeth and the state grew more Third World by the hour. At least, I thought, I could anticipate a reasonably stimulating football season. The Cowboys, I had guessed, were finally due a good season. In fact, their regular season opener against these expansion doo-dahs, the Houston Texans, was probably deep in the fourth quarter. It was still Sunday night in Texas.

A wholesome young gentleman was seated at a TV in the lounge watching European CNN news. He looked like somebody who might perhaps be rush captain for the SAEs at Vanderbilt. Scores from sporting events from every corner of the globe drifted across the bottom of the screen. His girlfriend, a pouty-faced blonde, was stylishly anorexic.

"Excuse me," I said, "but have they shown a score from the Cowboys-Texans game?"

"I don't care anything about American football. No one does," he shot back in a heavy French accent. I was stunned. Then he started speaking nasty-sounding Frog talk to his raisin-titted doll face, no doubt telling her what an asshole I was. She looked at me, rolling her eyes with contempt.

"Listen, you horse-face prick, I didn't ask you your opinion of American football. I just wanted to know if you knew the fucking score." That's what the guy who used to cover the Rangers would have said. And then he would have added, "So you aren't hip to American football, as opposed to the kind of football they play over here in these chickenshit little motor-scooter countries." Uh-uh. *No mas.* The contemporary me, the one who gets some

43

plum assignments from high-rent magazines, wasn't about to open his mouth and brand himself as the Ugly Texan.

No, I won't say a word. I'll just throw this glass of wine in his face, I was thinking. But then a score appeared on that TV screen, and another tacky Franco-American rift was avoided.

Dallas 19 . . . Houston 10.

Huh. Closer than I thought. No. Wait. The Houston team's score was highlighted in bright yellow, which designated the winning team. I had gotten it backward.

Dallas 10 . . . Houston 19.

Sacre merde! Maudite putain de con!

Down in the methane-shrouded bayous of Houston, the guy who edited the Texans' Web page, HoustonProFootball.com, was preparing this essay: "Well, well, well. The Dallas Cowboys. America's Team. What a pathetic joke. They're not even Texas's team. And at the rate they're sucking, before long, they won't even be Dallas's team. Eat it, losers."

Way to go, Cowboys. Way to go, Dave Campo. Way to go, Jerry Jones.

At that moment, I could not help but remember a conversation with Gil Brandt, the Cowboys' old super scout. Brandt was recalling the halcyon days of Tom Landry, back in the musty and distant past. That was when the Cowboys had a genuine head coach on the sidelines and not some crying clown who probably would be unable to hold down a job delivering telephone books because he couldn't handle the pressure.

"Why did Landry win so much?" Brandt had declared. "Because, while he would keep the team on an even keel over the course of a sixteen-game season, the one game that he would point to was the regular season opener. That was the one that counted most.

"Tom knew that, when you win the opener, it gave the rookies the message they were going to get involved in a winning tradition. And it got the media and fans in the right mood as well."

Brandt (this conversation happened in 2000) offered a statistic that fortified Landry's reasoning on the importance of winning that opener. Since they started playing the Super Bowl in January 1967, the teams that made the Super Bowl had an opening-game record of 57-7-2, and the teams that won the Super Bowl have—are you ready for this?—an opening-day record of 29-3-1. And what was Landry's opening-game record? Starting in 1965, he won seventeen straight. Seventeen straight! Nobody will ever equal that.

And how was that accomplished?

"In training camp." That's what I learned from Ernie Stautner, the man of iron, who coached Landry's defensive line for nearly three decades. "He'd take the team out to California for six weeks, and everything was geared to winning that opener. Those camps were tough, too. He made them that way, realizing that the players couldn't wait to get that over with and get on with the regular season."

So how had Campo's 2002 team prepared for the season opener? By devoting most of training camp to an appearance on reality TV. No, it wasn't *Joe Millionaire* or *The Bachelorette* or *Queer Eye for the Straight Guy*. It was the next worst thing—the HBO *Hardknocks* show, a presentation where the cameras were allowed backstage with a high-profile football team, on which the head coach himself sang his version of "My Babe." Great show, Dave. Let 'em know who's in charge.

"This comes from *Patton*," the coach explained. "You've got to get down with the troops. I felt like singing with the guys. That's getting down with the troops." Actually, Dave, the only time Patton ever got down with the troops was when he slapped the shit out of some shell-shocked soldier in a field hospital. If you want to entertain the troops, call Bob Hope. As for Dave, perhaps he should have transferred his act to the seniors division of *American Idol*. Simon would have hugged Campo.

Campo paraded in front of the cameras and made Knute Rockne speeches while his offensive line grew fatter and more out of shape by the day. The whole training camp was an indoor fiasco at the Alamodome in San Antonio, where the rock and heavy metal blaring over the PA system drowned out anything the coaches would yell at the players during the drill.

That is the foolproof formula for losing that opener that Landry deemed so vital and losing it to the ungodly likes of the Houston Texans, with a top draft pick rookie at quarterback and a remaining squad of fifty-two players who were waiver-wire material.

During the flight back across the Atlantic, I sat next to a woman who was getting actively loaded on Drambuie and telling me about how she was involved in some hush-hush Defense Department project in which they were pretty damn close to locating other life on some distant planet.

Ordinarily, I might have been compelled to press this woman, loaded or not, for details. But I simply could not get my mind off the Cowboys and their astonishingly humiliating, utterly disgusting loss to this Texans team, playing in that white-trash, bourbon-and-trombone city that gave the world Enron, where pro football never caught on because the rules of the sport were too complicated for the fan base. Okay, so Landry had a string of seventeen straight opening-game wins and would win twenty-one out of twenty-two before the spell wore off, while Campo's record was, let's see, 0 and 3.

Campo had arrived in Dallas with the Jimmy Johnson administration in 1989. Jimm-uh, as Jerry Jones used to call him, had been a product of Port Arthur, where a Texas Aggie will drive his date when she tells him to kiss her where it smells bad. He'd gone to high school with Janis Joplin. That Jones-Johnson partnership proved beyond a reasonable doubt that when two individuals who grew up on the outskirts of civilization achieve prosperity, turmoil is certain to ensue.

After Johnson had won his second straight Super Bowl, Jones had gotten blasted in a hotel bar in Orlando and told some reporters that he'd had a bellyful of Jimm-uh, that the coach's hairspray had destroyed the earth's ozone layer, and that Johnson was getting shit-canned. It's a shame that it was reported that Jones was plastered when he made that decision, because the consequences would soon cast all of us clearheaded drinkers, the wise and creative drinkers, in a poor light.

But Johnson was gone. His top defensive assistants had been leaving as well. Dave Wannestadt took the head coach's job with the Chicago Bears. Butch Davis abandoned the Cowboys to take over the Miami Hurricanes. Dave Campo became the beneficiary of these evacuations, advancing a notch with each departure. From assistant to the assistant, to a coordinator's post, and finally the head coach's position, after Jones fired Chan Gailey and was seemingly too fatigued at the time to instigate another external job search.

The Dave Campo regime shortly became a living-color illustration of what happens when the Peter Principle collides head-on with Murphy's Law. Since Campo was universally hailed as a "nice guy," he could also serve as Exhibit A to the Leo Durocher Doctrine—the one that mandates where nice guys will inevitably finish.

That debacle in Houston only brought to mind Dave Campo's world premiere as the Dallas Cowboys' head coach, the man in charge. I remember it vividly, because on the day of the opening game of Year 1 of the Campo Era, it was 111 degrees. And I remember that because the day before I had been serving as a "celebrity judge" in an outdoor event—the annual Labor Day goat cook-off in Brady, Texas. Here's a tip for you: If you ever have the opportunity to sample genuine, cedar-fed goat marinated in tubs of Lone Star beer and gently smoked for two days over mesquite coals by the world's most renowned goat cookers—don't.

So, with a greasy residue of charred goat still coating my tongue, it was rather surprising that the taste in my mouth could get any worse. But it did, watching as Dave Campo demonstrated his head-coaching skills for the first time at Texas Stadium. The Philadelphia Eagles lost the toss and began the game with an onside kick. What the hell kind of team would begin its regular season, playing on the road in what amounted to a blast furnace, with a daredevil stunt like an onside kick?

Well, that would be the kind of team that knew for certain that the opposition would be ill-prepared. So Andy Reid's Eagles recovered the kick and, after they stopped laughing, proceeded to slam the football down Dave Campo's gullet. Philadelphia scored. And scored again, and again. Troy Aikman left before halftime after suffering the next-to-last concussion of his career.

This time, Troy was lucky. He couldn't remember anything that happened during the Eagles fiasco.

On the Dallas sidelines, Campo's demeanor shifted from discombobulated to deranged. Back and forth. Dave shrieked in anguish. He flapped his wings. He was out of control. He somehow reminded me of a description of Ezra Pound: "His gestures and gyrations were those of someone trying to tell a deaf man that his house was on fire." The game was a complete and total rout from the first play on, and in the final minutes, Dallas receiver Joey Galloway suffered a season-ending knee injury.

Jerry Jones had seriously overpaid the Seattle Seahawks to attain Galloway's services. Dallas's first-round draft pick in 2002 *and* 2001 went sailing off to Starbucks country. What, then, was Galloway even doing on the field in the dying moments of a 40–14 Philadelphia butt-stomp? Why? Why? Campo really couldn't offer an answer. That established a postgame trend that earmarked the remainder of the man's dubious tenure, which was nothing more than a procession of strategic gaffes.

At Arizona: "Dave, you're behind seven points with a couple of minutes to play, you're within sight of the Cardinals' end zone, and you try a field goal (that missed). What good does the field goal do you even if you make it?"

At Texas Stadium, against Denver, on Thanksgiving: "Dave, you're down by sixteen, and then you make a touchdown with about six minutes to play. Why, at that point, did you not go for two? My fifth grader wants to know why you would do something so damn dumb. Why? Why?"

These postgame Q and A sessions with Campo had turned into uncomfortable spectacles for everybody involved. Lyndon Johnson used to complain about the same thing, when he'd endure the annual presidential roast staged by the Washington Press Club. LBJ had compared that to "the medieval rustics throwing shit at the village idiot."

Sometimes people have reasons for performing deeds that, in retrospect, might not have constituted acts of wisdom. Even the woman who got run over while attempting to walk across eight lanes of heavy, speeding traffic on the LBJ Freeway had an explanation for what she was thinking. From her bed in Parkland Hospital, she said she did it "to see if the Lord was with me." If blundering Dave Campo had presented that rationale at any of his postgame excuse fests, it might have won him some fan support, at least.

It might be said of Dave Campo that of all of the head coaches in the entire annals of the National Football League, he stood head and shoulders above all others when it came to a total and absolute absence of what military historians refer to as "command presence." Here was a man who was clearly *not* born to lead. While his Cowboys teams appalled their fans and amused their foes with a ghastly and unending presentation of blown assignments, misfires, screwups, dropped balls, mindless penalties, and botched opportunities, Campo performed anguished backflips on the sidelines.

Dallas fans from past years used to rag on Tom Landry for what they perceived as his lack of fire and passion in critical moments in key games. True, Landry appeared bored, like a man in church, hungry for lunch, glancing at his watch and wondering if the preacher would ever shut up. "That was because Landry realized that there was nothing he could do about the play that was just over. He was thinking about the next play and the play after that." Mike Ditka told me that shortly before Landry died.

Even the everlastingly benign play-by-play guy Pat Summerall, who always left the negative stuff to his color announcer, was moved to note on the air that "Dave Campo's posture on the sideline, when things go badly, is hardly the thing that would inspire confidence from his players." Campo, to his credit, attracted comparisons to some of the most outstanding characters in television drama.

He reminded many of Jerry Van Dyke's Luther Van Dam, the goofy sidekick of Hayden Fox on the comedy series *Coach*. To others, Campo revived fond memories of Ralph Kramden, just before he would offer to send Alice to the moon. In a state that treasures high school football—and that's the echelon of the sport that attracts the majority of fans in Texas who truly qualify as esoteric—Campo's shortcomings were even more magnified. If Dave Campo had been coaching in, say, Brownwood, Texas, the season ticket holders would have nailed him to the cross atop the steeple of the East Side Assembly of God.

No, from a won-lost standpoint, the Dave Campo teams were not the worst in the NFL. But they were the shittiest. When it came to fat, dumb, and lazy, these Dallas Cowboys would know no equals. Two games at Texas Stadium punctuated the Dave Campo era as head coach of the Dallas Cowboys. Both were against the team's arch nemesis from the old and by now nearly forgotten days when Super Bowls had been a priority around North Texas, the San Francisco 49ers.

In 2001 Terrell Owens snared a TD pass from Jeff Garcia in a game that was already a blowout. Owens, being Owens, chose not to perform his celebratory war dance in the end zone. Rather, he raced back to the fifty-yard line and performed a swell impersonation of Gene Kelly's big scene in *Singin' in the Rain,* tap-dancing on the Cowboys' symbolic star painted onto the turf at midfield. Cowboys defensive back George Teague raced to the scene of sacrilege and delivered a forearm in the direction of Owens's head.

Two years after the fact, Teague, who was once described by a teammate as "looking like that devil you see on the label of hot sauce bottles," would reflect on what happened. "Kareem Larimore was covering Owens one-on-one, so it was obvious to me that Owens would score, and I figured he would perform something outlandish—and so I was ready in advance to respond."

After Teague knocked Owens on his ass, a melee involving both benches naturally followed. The whole tawdry scene looked like a failed bit on WWF's Thursday night *Smackdown*. Under the Jones-Campo amalgamation, the Cowboys had fallen from an NFL juggernaut to a burlesque routine, a warm-up act for the fan dancer.

A year later, the 49ers were back. For most of the afternoon, the 49ers appeared to have left their hearts in San Francisco. It was December 10, and despite being a playoff contender, the 'Niners had been strangely noncombatant.

As the two-minute warning approached, the Cowboys led by 3 and faced third down and only a yard at the San Francisco twenty-nine-yard line. One more first down, and the game belonged to Dallas. It was imperative that Dallas maintain control of the ball because the defense was gassed. San Francisco had scored with ease on its previous possession. Also, the Cowboys, because of an injury to Mario Edwards, had a cornerback on the field, Dwayne Goodrich, who was even more inept than Kareem Larimore.

A sideline microphone picked up Dave Campo's voice. "Two

plays to make one yard. Let's do it!" Emmitt Smith, on the first play, gained one-half of the one yard that was all that the Cowboys needed. Fourth and a half yard, and now the microphone again registered Campo's words. Apparently, he was speaking to his special teams coach, Joe Avazanno, "What do I do now?"

What he did was send the field goal unit onto the field. Even if the kick was good, Dallas would yield the ball to San Francisco with two minutes to play—and Dwayne Goodrich out there to cover, yes, that tacky Terrell Owens. Campo, by attempting the kick, had created a lose-lose situation for the Cowboys. Billy Cundiff missed the forty-seven-yarder, and Garcia actually let the clock run down to close to 0:00 before casually tossing the game-winning TD to Owens while Goodrich watched from somewhere in the next county.

Up in heaven, Tom Landry looked at Vince Lombardi, shook his head in disgust, and wandered off to harp practice. Don Shula was turning in his grave, and he wasn't even dead yet.

Elsewhere, in a luxury suite in Texas Stadium, a light suddenly switched on in Jerry Jones's attic. For the past three years, an entire locker-roomful of players, abetted by an officeful of dysfunctional coaching personnel, had been picking Jerry's pockets, stealing his groceries, and siphoning his gasoline. Nowhere in the landscape of professional sport could one locate a more overcompensated yet uninspired, underachieving team, more complacent in its ineptitude than the Dallas Cowboys. Jones was writing the big checks, evidently oblivious to the ripoff.

Then, watching Terrell Owens catch the winning TD pass, shimmy, shake, and spike the ball between Dwayne Goodrich's feet, Jerry suddenly snapped.

While the media gathered outside the Cowboys' dressing

room awaiting yet the latest entry in Dave Campo's expanding tome of lame postgame explanations, Jones walked past and said to nobody in particular, perhaps just talking to himself: "That was the stupidest fuckin' bunch of goddamn horseshit I have ever seen!"

Stupidest bunch of goddamn horseshit—by Jerry's standards, that was a rare demonstration of eloquence. None of his customary mixed metaphors, no mangled participles, no tortured syntax. Best of all, Jerry was being sincere.

To the Dallas fans in their suffering, that was the most gratifying declaration since Jimmy Johnson jumped up in the locker room after beating the 49ers in the 1992 NFC championship game and yelled out, "How 'bout them Cowboys!"

Listed along with the New York Yankees and Manchester United, the pride of the British Empire, the Cowboys still ranked among the most recognizable franchises in the world. Now Jerry Jones realized that the time had come to burn the thing down and start over. When it comes to swallowing one's pride, the meal is not so unpalatable when one's pocketbook is at stake.

In a fortnight, Jones would stand before the media, and therefore the free world as it exists in North Texas, and bid farewell to Dave Campo. It was the same old Jerry, laying it on with thick applications of maudlin hokiness, like listening to somebody's great-aunt play "A Drunkard's Grave" in the parlor on the Hammond organ.

Poor old Dave. As a Christmas gift to his assistants, most of whom would be receiving their exit visas along with the head coach himself, Campo had presented each with a Dallas Cowboys helmet. Attached to the helmet was a plaque, on which Coach Dave offered his appreciation for their loyalty. What a peculiar parting gesture. It was something akin to the captain of the *Titanic* honoring his crew with ice cubes inscribed "Thanks for the Memories."

"There's never been anyone who's worked harder, been more diligent, been more loyal and more enthusiastic than Dave Campo," Jerry Jones told the media.

In other words, see ya later, asshole, 'cause the Tuna's coming to Texas.

CHAPTER 5

"YA KNOW, I COULD WORK FOR A GUY LIKE THAT"

The America that we behold now four years deep into the twenty-first century, according to the incumbent executive administration, is locked in the embrace of a sonic-boom economy. One cannot deny that the U.S. workforce has been energized by the emergence of three growth industries that demonstrate no future indications of a recessional ebb: breaking, entering, and motivational speaking. These are jobs that cannot be easily outsourced to foreign soil.

Television programmers highlight the CEOs of those first two professions on presentations such as *COPS*. In order to catch the third category in action on public TV, the viewer must wait past the midnight hours to catch the motivators at work. You can find the motivators on what are called advertorials, usually on the B-side of the cable schedule.

They're fun to watch, some of them, usually offering a message more easily comprehensible than the televangelists, who are prone to lapse into abstractions that many viewers, already stoked with the rapture that comes from various intoxicants and inhalants, find confoundingly impossible to grasp. Also troublesome is the fact that so many of the occupants of the TV pulpit favor the full-blown and heavily lacquered hairstyle that would eventually become the undoing of Jimmy Johnson as a National Football League sideline personality.

No, in the estimation of this writer, the motivators, who implore their audiences to dig deeply within in order to locate their genuine financial selves, offer some damn good points. Eschewing the obscure syntax found in the fundamentalist scriptures, the motivators come straight at the viewers with sharply edged acronyms like TIGER and BADASS. I was especially impressed with a point hammered home by an old codger who had overcome an involuntary blinking problem and amassed a huge personal fortune selling weight-loss cookies that also cure pattern baldness.

The key to selling these cookies, he said, or any other product from term life insurance to bronzed baby shoes, was essentially tied to the axiom dealing with the early bird and the worm. He said that rich people, who are natural marketing targets for anybody attempting to make a living in direct sales, tend to be eccentric. The richer they come, the weirder they get, the motivator said.

These rich eccentrics share certain characteristics. They sleep on the floor, are obsessed with a desire to invent a perpetual-motion machine, and, most important, are always, without exception, big breakfast eaters. (Here, the man could only have been describing Jerry Jones, a morning person if there ever was one. During those Super Bowl years, Jerry was frequently seen all over town at 3:00 A.M., rockin' and rollin'.)

Forget taking the client for the expensive dinner, the motivator said. Even if you make the sale, the client will be sluggish on an overpriced meal and loaded on even more hideously overpriced wine, and at arrival of the new day, will have forgotten that he or she had agreed to the deal in the first place.

No. Catch them at breakfast, which is the apex of the day for the people empowered to write the checks. The good salespeople will schedule as many as three power breakfasts on a given morning. One at 6:00 A.M., another at 7:30 A.M., and still a third around 9:00 A.M, if they can possibly work it in. So by the time the always-a-stagehand-but-never-a-star go-getter is settling down at his desk, the *real* salesperson will already have two, maybe three checks stuck in his or her pocket and will pleasantly devote the remainder of the day to going fishing, getting laid, or both.

Amplifying his point, the motivator issued some wisdom that should capture the attention of any student of human nature. These eccentric rich people, the ones who have the capacity to sign the checks, come geared with a naturally imbued self-defense system that is geared around the chronic use of the word "no." So when it comes to the successful conclusion of a spiel, the salesman must then bring forth the proposition: "So? Can you think of any sound business reason why we shouldn't do this deal?" Thus, the elimination of the rich guy's natural inclination to respond with a negative.

But then, just as this man who learned to channel his obsessive blinking problem into a beguiling personality asset, right at the point that he had convinced me to hawk my typewriter and enroll in his seminar, he lost me. He changed course from the commonsense approach and directed this manifesto to those career dead-enders. "Keep your antenna up," the motivator demanded, "because what you are seeking is seeking you!"

Horseshit. For a quarter of a century, I had been avidly attempting to sell the greatest screenplay ever written, *Confessions of a Teenaged Chiropractor*. I have sent copies, with the recommended self-addressed, postage-paid return envelope containing the work, to MGM, Universal, Disney, Warner Brothers, et al., and they were returned all right—unopened. I changed my tactics and quit prepaying the postage, but Dreamworks and HBO sent it back anyway.

Phone calls to Robert Altman, Woody Allen, Kevin Costner, Mel Gibson, and even Bruce Willis have received no response. Stanley Kubrick did express a mild interest, but when he died, so did my hopes and dreams. So, I am sorry, Mr. Motivational Speaker. What I was seeking sure as hell was not seeking me.

Then—although it's far too late to salvage my career—I saw what individuals of far greater ambition and accomplishment than most of us have, can make happen when they raise their so-called antennae. Bill Parcells and Jerry Jones. At the outset of the 2002 football season, both men were seeking something—albeit neither could have realized at the time that it would be each other. So this antenna theory, bizarre as it might seem on surface examination, was exactly the feature involved in the gradual unfolding of the strangest success story that football, professional or otherwise, has witnessed since Tom Dempsey of the New Orleans Saints kicked the longest field goal in league history (at the time) with an artificial foot.

Jones's plight was clear enough after his Cowboys lost that
season opener to the Houston Texans. That was simply the most
dumbfoundingly disturbing loss in the history of the franchise.
Screw the Ice Bowl. Forget Super Bowl V, when the Cowboys
got shafted by some hallucinatory zebra who called a phantom
fumble on the goal line and allowed Baltimore to eventually win
the game, 16–13. Forget that play that has been memorialized as
"The Catch," that blind toss that Joe Montana heaved to Dwight
Clark at the back of the end zone in the 1981 championship
game that will gall Dallas fans into and beyond eternity. None of
those generated the collective pall that crossed North Texas after
the Cowboys had been beaten by the first-year expansion Texans,
a game that will be historically recorded in the annals of Valley
Ranch as the Barium Enema on the Bayou.

That was more than a football game because the outcome
clearly established that Big D, for all of its worldly pretensions,
had been relegated to the sorry position of second tier, not just
globally and nationally but within the state of Texas as well. This
loss to those Houston Texans, whoever in the hell they were supposed to be, simply served as the final punctuation of a civic
downspiral, a positioning of rapid decline, that first afflicted Dallas in the mid-1980s. When the oil-producing nations of the sand
lands decreed that the value of fossil fuels would be ordained by
the mandates of a free and open market, the Big D economy was
at once clotheslined by a chain reaction. When the petro boys hit
the skids, the local banks shut down, and the real estate people,
like starving sheep, joined the parade to the poorhouse. Fact was,
most of the high-profile big spenders around Dallas, the ones
driving their white Rolls-Royces with sterling silver trailer hitches
and snorting mounds of cocaine in their Learjets en route to

Vegas, were seriously overextended in the first place. When the Camel People pulled their mean-spirited practical joke that rendered a barrel of oil less valuable than a can of diet Pepsi, the collapse was a horrid thing to watch. Said one leading Dallas economist, "It was like you're already walking down the street naked, and all of sudden, the cops drive up."

The emerging social force in Dallas became the Nouveau Broke. Gradually, the city dug its way through some semblance of a comeback, mostly on the impetus of a software-based economy, but every backwoods hick venue in the land, from Bangor to Bakersfield, could claim the same thing. The swagger that was the trademark of the ultra-rich Dallas oilman—that was gone forever.

Area pride experienced something of a revival when the J Brothers, Johnson and Jones, pieced together their Super Bowl spree, but that faded soon enough.

Big D's reputation had declined to a nadir in that the city was not even acceptable as a stopover for Vince McMahon's hired goons from pro wrestling. At a WWF event in the summer of 2000 at Reunion Arena, crammed so full of the products of Wal-Mart America that you couldn't see the aisles, a wrestler called Edge stood in the ring with a microphone and orated the following: "Well, here we are in Dallas. You know, the president got shot here one time. Some people think one guy shot him. Some people think a bunch of guys shot him. But I know what happened. He took one look at this shit pile and committed suicide!" That short speech was greeted with some boos, and that was followed by a chorus that sang, "A-s-s-h-o-l-e! A-s-s-h-o-l-e!" But nobody rioted or attempted to lynch the guy.

The final charade that Dallas could rank alongside the great metropolitan settings of the planet was cruelly placed on display when various civic enthusiasts—with strong convictions and sur- prisingly straight faces—decided to forge a serious bid to land the 2012 Summer Olympic Games.

Talk about blind faith. When tacky questions were asked such as, "Where will the mountain bike competition be con- ducted?" and "What is the anticipated death rate among the marathon runners, since that event will take place in 112-degree heat?" the boosters provided can-do answers like, "Shit, we'll just build some mountains" and "Haven't those marathoners ever heard of air-conditioning?"

Perhaps an omen was involved with the timing of a massive pep rally at Fair Park, staged to seduce the U.S. Olympic site se- lection committee to throw in with Dallas. That event was scheduled for the afternoon of September 11, 2001. It was only a matter of a couple of weeks that the committee's short list of candidates for the 2012 games was to be formally announced. Dallas wasn't on it. More embarrassingly, Houston—which had made a halfhearted effort to secure the games—remained in the running. That was bad enough. The Cowboys' loss to this pseudo NFL team that they called the Texans—that was the very worst. Despite the Enron debacle that identified Houston as quite the fraud in its own right, it was firmly established that Dallas was destined to subordinate its role to South Texas for years and per- haps decades to come.

A photograph of Jerry Jones, trudging off the field while the celebrating nobodies in their Texans uniforms appeared to be laughing at the beleaguered Cowboys owner, spoke more elo- quently than all of the volumes of Shakespeare when it came to the inherent tragicomic nature that is the plight of the human species. During the 1960s, I was amused to read a newspaper account of a man who attended the homecoming bonfire of a high school largely attended by the lake trash that lives north of Fort Worth. This man's enjoyment of that local cultural event was tempered somewhat when he noticed that what that very morning had been his living room furniture was helping to fuel the pep rally blaze. I tried to imagine the look on that poor schmuck's face as he watched his sofa and coffee table go up in smoke, and I finally saw it at last—in the expression that crossed Jerry Jones's reconstructed countenance at the conclusion of that 2002 opening game in Houston.

From Jones's point of view, something of greater sentimental value than his home furnishings was lost in those flames. If you want to see tears in Jerry Jones's eyes, simply rupture his bank account. The corniest cliché in all of sports is the one that goes, "There's no 'I' in the word 'team.'" But there are several in "multimillionaire," which has always been Jerry's most cherished identity. Ticket sales, luxury-box sales, corporate sponsorships—those will dwindle after too much on-the-field ineptitude, even if (or particularly if) that team happens to be the Dallas Cowboys. At this phase of Jerry's master strategy for the evolution of his franchise, even more was at stake. Jerry had already been studying the blueprints for the eventual new stadium that would house his team. This was more than a stadium—it was a retail development complex and a theme park.

This would be Jerry's legacy to North Texas long after he was dead and gone to wherever guys like him wind up: the structural wonder that all of Texas would recognize as Jonestown.

The pressing concerns were where to put it and which of the various civic entities in the region known as the Metroplex would help finance it. With yet another crappy team and Jones's fourth straight season without a chance at achieving the playoffs, Jonestown was looming as a more distinct reality. "I was afraid," Jones would confide later. "I always just assumed we were going to win football games. If we fell short of contending, I was sure it was temporary—we'd correct that within months. That's the deal I have with our fans and our constituencies. They know that Jones will get it done, and they'll give him the benefit of the doubt. But we hadn't been getting it done for three years in a row. I felt like I'd lost a lot of my benefit-of-the-doubt collateral."

So Jerry Jones's antenna was suddenly up and fully activated, transmitting an SOS heard round the pro football world.

Back east, the Tuna prepared for his third consecutive season of self-imposed exile.

Big Bill was trying his dead-level best to entertain and inform the viewers of ESPN. But just as stonemasons for some reason make mediocre bricklayers and so-called gonzo sportswriters fail miserably when it comes to writing television commercials for banks, former football coaches, with the singular exception of John Madden, were simply not naturals when it came to performing on-screen.

Parcells was born to give the world his talents as the Jock Whisperer, remember, the man with the rarest of gifts which enables him to penetrate the subconscious of the world's most gifted athletes (outside of the ones in the NBA, of course) and produce an alloy forged of fire and fear and focus that results in the creation of the team-obsessed Super Jock.

As with Far Eastern mystics who self-levitate and walk through walls, it is the bane of the life of the Whisperer that when removed from his individually unique specialties, attempts at a conventional existence present clumsy complications.

For Exhibit A, let me present the saga of Elbert "Muscles" Foster. Muscles—unlike Robert Redford's hokey, movie-land, enrobed-in-self-love presentation—was a real-life, honest-to-God horse whisperer, celebrated as the greatest that the state of Texas had ever seen. Muscles was the trainer of the great Cutter Bill, a golden stallion that dominated national cutting-horse competition for over a decade in the 1960s and the '70s. The horse, owned by Rex Cauble, a standard-issue, megabucks Texas oilman-rancher, traveled to competitions in his own specially equipped aircraft. But everybody in the horse world knew that Cutter Bill owed his reputation to the trainer, Muscles Foster.

Unfortunately, Muscles would deviate from his given calling, that of the whisperer. In order to raise extra bucks, Muscles devised a scheme in which he transported prostitutes from the Texas Gulf Coast to Colombia in shrimp boats, where he traded the girls for high-grade marijuana. What a scheme. The federal prison population was greatly enriched by Muscles's non-whisperer endeavors, and he died broke and crazy.

This is not to suggest that laboring as an on-air personality at ESPN is quite as over the top as transporting dope and pussy in shrimp boats. In the minds of some, including perhaps Parcells himself, it might have come close. How much fun could the Tuna have been having, commenting on the grandeur of the accomplishments of his former defensive assistant, Bill Belichick, now head coach of the defending Super Bowl champion New England Patriots?

Belichick and the Tuna had parted on less than cordial terms. It had been understood, or at least by Parcells, that Belichick would replace him as head coach when he walked away from the Jets job in 1999. In fact, Belichick had taken a $1 million bonus from the late Jets owner, the man whom Parcells would think of as a surrogate father, Leon Hess, allegedly based on the stipulation that Belichick would stick around to run things after the Tuna's eventual departure. Instead, Belichick would leave the Jets and take over with the Tuna's old outfit, the Patriots. Parcells felt betrayed. And he would say so in his book. "I'm still not happy with Belichick," he wrote. "I don't know how you can take a million dollars to stay another year to become head coach and then walk out on the job. Nothing he has said since about what happened makes any sense to me."

So what if the Pats were beyond lucky to have advanced even to the AFC finals, after a referee made the most controversial and universally criticized ruling since the O. J. Simpson not-guilty verdict when he ruled a Tom Brady fumble an incompletion in the game-altering play against the Oakland Raiders.

Belichick was the toast of the pro-coaching profession now. And Parcells? He was just toast.

The widely held presumption indicated that the role of the broadcast golden-throat was to be the Tuna's lifetime assignment. He'd admitted as much in his memoir of his 1999 exit campaign with the New York Jets, the one that he'd authored with the collaboration assistance of the late Will McDonough entitled *The Final Season . . . My Last Year as a Head Coach in the NFL*. He couldn't have made it plainer than that. It looked as if he was about to renege on the statement when he agreed to take over the Tampa Bay Bucs prior to the 2002 season, then backed out of that agreement.

"Case closed," crowed the Tuna-watchers of the mass media.

Why would the man even consider going back to the grind? Even Parcells's recent ex-wife of thirty-nine years, Judy, had told *60 Minutes* that during the football season, her husband was chronically "miserable, anxious, exasperated, and depressed." She'd said that during Bill's so-called "last year as a head coach" with the Jets. To that, Parcells had responded, "Well, first of all, this is no disrespect to my wife, Judy, because she's been in this for a long time, but Judy doesn't know whether the ball is blown up or stuffed with feathers. Okay? But right now, she'd be accurate in her assessment."

So the 2002 season rocked along with Tampa Bay and Philadelphia clearly emerging as the top teams of the NFC. The Raiders, aging as they were, were ranked as the best bet to claim the championship of the other conference.

It was mid-December when Bill Parcells sat in the ESPN studio, reviewing tapes and preparing for a telecast with one of his on-the-air colleagues, Chris Mortensen, when some footage of Jerry Jones appeared on one of the screens.

"Ya know? I could work for a guy like that," Parcells said to Mortensen, who recalls nearly falling out of his chair. In the book that Parcells had written about the 1999 ordeal with the Jets, the Tuna had flatly stated that a guy like Jerry Jones was the last person in the world he would work for. Look at this passage, dated December 23. It's well before game time, Jets versus Dallas at Texas Stadium, and Parcells is walking around the field. "I look across and see the Dallas trainer and another guy working out some injured players. I see one of them is Larry

Allen, who is the best offensive lineman in the league. He hasn't been playing for them the last couple of weeks, and I sure as hell hoped he wasn't going to be ready for us.

"But this is the thing that surprised and disturbed me. The other guy working out the injured players is Jerry Jones, the team owner. Now I've never seen that anywhere in my life, the owner working out injured players to see if they are ready to go or not. On most teams, one of the assistant coaches will work out the injured player, then they come back to the head coach and tell him what the deal is going to be.

"Jerry Jones, from what I was led to believe that day talking to some of the Dallas people, is very involved. I know at one time he played college ball and coached a kids team or something like that, but the NFL is supposed to be a little bit different. They tell me that Jerry has a phone in his box that goes directly to the bench, and he'll call during the game with some message. Or if he wants to talk to certain players about their performance.

"If an owner wants to come around during the week and encourage the players, root for them and let them know he is with them, that's fine with me. But once the owner wants to coach, I'd be out of there the next day. I couldn't coach in that situation myself."

Now, here is the Tuna telling Chris Mortensen that he could work for a guy like that.

If Bill Parcells belonged to a group that we might call, say, Coach-a-holics Anonymous, then this would be the day the Tuna might concede was the one when he hit rock bottom.

When Mortensen asked the Tuna what the hell was going through his mind, Parcells responded, "He wants to win. If you ever talk to him, give him my cell phone number."

The next week, Mortensen, indeed, was talking with Jerry Jones, preparing for an ESPN piece about Emmitt Smith. He mentioned to Jones that Parcells had expressed an interest in talking coaching but did not offer the cell phone number. The rest was up to Jerry Jones.

Within a few short days, Jones and Parcells were sitting in Jerry's private jet, parked on a New Jersey airstrip, and discussing the future. Other than the parties involved in the conversation, nobody would seriously dare to consider that Bill Parcells would be prowling Jones's sideline.

But hidden clues suggested otherwise. In the Tuna's weekly column that he wrote for NFL.com, in his little "quick hits" sidebar, Parcells made the following observations:

- Dallas will have a good defense next year.
- Cowboys safety Roy Williams reminds me of a young Ronnie Lott.

Those comments appeared in the December 11 edition of NFL.com, the same week that Parcells had suggested to Mortensen that he could work for a guy like Jones.

Here's another item. It is not widely known that Bill Parcells's actual name is not Bill at all. It's Duane. Duane Charles Parcells.

Look in *The Texas Almanac* and you will learn the following:

- Official Texas State Motto—Friendship.
- Official Texas State Tree—Pecan.
- Official Texas State Bird—Mockingbird.
- Official Texas First Name—Duane.

Another backstage factor that could be deemed a key in attracting Bill Parcells to locate to a warmer climate: In the lonely aftermath of his divorce, Parcells, according to some gossipmongers, had developed a fondness for a special woman who lived in the Dallas area.

Before Jerry Jones and the Tuna ever got around to discussing items like salary and length of the contract—both will insist those topics never arose inside of Jones's jet—the deal was done.

CHAPTER 6

THAT OLD-MAN SMELL

More than anything, media professionals crave a natural disaster. A killer tornado, unlike the mayor and the chief of police, won't look you in the eye and tell lies until sundown. The mudslide won't bore you into a sobbing hysteria with details of its redistricting plan. The earthquake, unlike the CEO who just skipped down with the pension, won't threaten to sue the reporter who describes the extent of the carnage and devastation that it's wrought.

Here's an example. In 1988 a Category 5 hurricane named Gilbert was bearing down oh so ominously on the Texas Gulf Coast. The potential for the persons who gathered and presented the news was unlimited. Hurricane Gilbert had the Brownsville-South Padre Island area squarely in its crosshairs. This booger offered the capacity to rumble northward and flood the entire Rio Grande Valley. Or better yet, it might then veer up along the coastline and wipe out Corpus Christi as well, while thousands would be swept away by surging salt water. The Galveston hurricane of 1900 killed more people than the Chicago Fire and Johnstown Flood combined. Oh, this was going to be a doozy.

TV reporters were dispatched to the area in droves, rejoicing at the notion of appearing on camera with the wind whipping at the lapels of their trench coats as the surf thundered behind them, signaling the dreadful arrival of a menacing monster from the sea. One-hundred-and-eighty-mile-an-hour winds! Twelve-foot tides! Jesus Christ, what a party this was going to be.

But Gilbert would betray them. Suddenly, the storm decided to turn left, cut into the jungles of the Yucatán, peter out, and die. The working press was appalled. Here, they were all primed to cover the disaster of the century, and all they got was a bunch of drowned monkeys.

Dan Rather, quaking and livid at his anchor desk at CBS News, actually called the National Weather Service and cussed out a meteorologist for misforecasting the Big Blow. Shit, now he'd have to return to the dreariness of the stretch of the Bush-Dukakis presidential campaign. What a drag.

In the newsroom of a major North Texas paper, desk drawers were slammed and wastebaskets were kicked. A city editor stood and screamed, "What's the matter with that fucking hurricane!"

So now that you fully comprehend the core motivation of the modern working journalist, you can understand the zeal with which the media reacted to the bizarre bulletin just in from the sports desk. Bill Parcells, the autocratic Tuna who recognizes no higher authority in the universe than himself when it comes to the operational control of a football team, was going to work for Jerry Jones, the micromanaging pigskin pooh-bah, otherwise known as the Sultan of Twat.

Now we're talking. All of the elements are precisely in place for the Perfect Storm, a genuine Sebastian Junger wet dream.

At first, the voices within the media could not accept the fact that the union would take place. Reporters, the kind who work for editors who not only thrive on controversy but demand it of their field hands even if it has to be manufactured, these people don't get that lucky. If they had been born to be lucky, they would have gone to Yale and joined the DKE fraternity. ARE YOU KIDDING ME? *Sports Illustrated* bellowed in a crimson headline. This was after the Jones-Parcells tête-à-tête in Jerry's jet plane, parked at the Teeterboro airport.

When Tex Schramm, representing the National Football League, and Lamar Hunt, the envoy for the rival American Football League, initiated their historic 1966 discussion that would quickly lead to a merger of the two organizations and the creation of what would become the Super Bowl, where did they convene to start the peace talks? At the most conspicuous location imaginable, the base of the statue of the Texas Ranger, inscribed ONE RIOT—ONE RANGER, the centerpiece of the lobby at Dallas Love Field, which was the principal airport in North Texas at the time. At least, that's what Schramm told me, and after a few travelers in the crowded lobby offered curious stares, they retired to Hunt's car, outside in the short-term public parking lot.

But in the modern era of mass media, when Jones and Parcells staged what was arranged as a hush-hush tryst, the walls had eyes and ears. Initial reports—throughout Texas, at least—were etched with disbelief, if not out-and-out denial. Columnists for what used to be remembered as the "big-time metropolitan dailies" were finally agreeing that Dave Campo, the nice guy, had to go. Yet these writers, supplied with operatives bringing word from within Jerry Jones's hidden corporate chambers, were insisting in print that Norv Turner, former Cowboys offensive coordinator during Troy Aikman's gilded age, could, should, and would be the next head coach in Dallas.

After Parcells—later the same night of his daytime session with Jones at the airport—had gone on ESPN with Chris Mortensen and all but flatly declared that "if Jerry wants me, I'll go," the media remained beyond skeptical. "One chance in 100," thundered one writer. Hell, Jerry would bring back Barry Switzer before he'd bring in a "there's one boss around here and you're looking at him" figure like Parcells. Besides, hadn't Parcells enlisted to take charge of the Tampa Bay Bucs just a year before, only to jilt the team after the engagement had been sealed with everything but a kiss? If the Tuna would turn down an organization fully supplied with all the talent and residual details already in place to drive to the Super Bowl and then win the thing, why would he instead turn to Dallas, now the home of scattered pro football debris, where the decline of talent and discipline had left the franchise in a condition that was a hybrid of the Arena League and the XFL? What they hadn't considered was that Parcells's professional head-coaching reputation was based entirely upon taking charge of what the home improvement people call fixer-uppers, the decaying structures in neighborhoods that were fashionable when the trolleys used to run, and transforming the pigsty into the mansion on the hill. Hell, anybody, even a punk like Jon Gruden, could win a championship with the material in place at Tampa. How would that enhance the Hall of Fame legend of Bill Parcells? This mess in Dallas, now that was the challenge for a *real* coach.

The Cowboys job presented an additional allure to Parcells, and he articulated that. "Out in Vegas, they have what they call the lounge acts, and then they have the Big Room people, and in the NFL, the Cowboys are definitely a Big Room act," he'd said. He was correct in that regard. The Tampa Bay Bucs could win every Super Bowl game played for the next decade, and they'd still be a lounge act. Parcells, hopefully, was mindful of another ominous reality. The Big Room can bring on dreadful consequences. Look what it did to Elvis. And Liberace. And more recently, Roy Horn, who was a tiger whisperer until the tiger whispered back.

On the Wednesday after the Saturday meeting in New Jersey, Parcells contacted his TV coworker Mortensen and confirmed to him that Jones, or his representatives, and the Tuna's agent, Jimmy Sexton, had agreed to the terms of a contract worth $17.1 million. Parcells said, "I'm going to do it. It's going to happen."

That was when the reality of the event struck home, to Mortensen, the media, and the world in general.

The reality of Parcells's job change was also noticed at ESPN, where his abrupt departure to Dallas caused complications. He was supposed to work the playoffs but instead gave in, yielding again to his addiction to the sideline. Now ESPN was stuck without a guy. The migratory work habits of various ex-coaches and their attraction to returning to the game is a growing concern at all the networks. That activity would have a carryover effect on another personality with North Texas ties. When former Texas

Rangers manager Bobby Valentine was fired by the New York Mets and took a job at ESPN similar to Parcells's, the network was careful to place provisions in his contract that might prevent him from repeating Parcells's hasty exit. Otherwise, Valentine might have skipped the series to go off and manage in some place like Panama. As it was, Bobby V. worked through his contract and sped off to Japan. But nobody outside the realm of network TV gave a shit about any of that—the Tuna and Jones act was about to take center stage.

Oh, goody. Hot damn. Every person even remotely familiar with the up-to-date scripting of the ongoing daytime serial known as the NFL joined in a Greek chorus and, in perfect harmony, yodeled an aria entitled "I'll Bet You a Case of Beer That This Marriage Won't Last Fifteen Minutes."

The eruption might not have come instantaneously, but it would be happening soon enough. Jerry and the Tuna, staging a rumble in the boiler room. Who do you like in that one? The Tuna maintains a size advantage, but Jones, you know for certain, will have an ice pick and a bowie knife concealed in his boot. That's how they do things in Arkansas, and that's how every aspiring billionaire always does business. Hold on, though. The Tuna's from Jersey, you know, and as soon as Jerry produces the blade, then Parcells, proud son of the Garden of Freight Docks, will counter, swinging a gym sock loaded with lug nuts. The Thrill-a In Manila with be chapel service compared with this jamboree.

Ten years before, fifteen certainly, those prognostications probably would have been correct. As men in their forties, Parcells and Jones were in lockstep in their seething inner drive to establish themselves in a professional universe, impetuous clones who heeded their own inner voices, propelled by a paranoid-level distrust of any external influences that might stand in their way.

That was then. When a man approaches, and then surpasses, his sixtieth birthday, an experience that both coach and owner had lately endured, vast changes occur.

Parcells and Jones belong to the most forgotten of America's generations. These are the individuals who lie between *The Greatest Generation*, those people immortalized in Tom Brokaw's book who survived the Depression and won the war, and the illustrious Baby Boomers, who grew up to become the greatest legion of consumers the world has yet known but otherwise never accomplished a goddamn thing.

So let's call the lost children of the Parcells-Jones era the Bomber Boomers; in other words, the people who were alive when Hiroshima happened. These are people who are old enough to remember when television was largely unknown to American households, and their most extravagant form of childhood entertainment was not playing *Grand Theft Auto* on PlayStation 2 but reading ten-cent Little Lulu comic books.

Oh, the changes these Bomber Boomers have witnessed in their lifetimes, technological and sociological upheaval that might be unprecedented in all of history. With a suddenness that was startling, the Bomber Boomers watched as the American mind-set shifted from *Enola Gay* to openly gay.

Things happen to the man crossing that age sixty barrier, the last chapter of male menopause, when, without the aid of newly discovered medical additives, the biological cock ceases to tick. As Jack LaLanne's young wife pointed out so succinctly: "We have sex almost every night. Almost on Monday . . . almost on Tuesday . . ."

The symptoms of psychiatric turmoil that characterize the traumatic morning that comes after the fiftieth-birthday party— those disappear, only to be replaced by orthopedic ones. The skeletal structure shrinks in direct proportion with the elongation of the nutsack. You are obsolete. Actuarial charts, compounded by tens of thousands of marketing surveys, have confirmed it. All of those Super Bowl ads, in case you don't know it, are targeted entirely toward the eighteen-to-thirty-five demographic. Wait a minute, the sixty-year-old will argue. Hold your horses. Not so fast. "I've got more disposable income than these snot-nosed brats—and I buy computer products, SUVs, and cold beer just like they do."

Maybe so, Pop. But you still don't matter. At sixty, even with the blessing of great genes and good health, you're late into the third quarter of the game of life, you're seventeen points behind, and you're still running the Wishbone T. Everything that you thought you loved is gone now. Your parents have died, and all the closest friends of your youth, your old running buddies, they're all either dead, too, or in prison, or on the run.

The real killer is not involved with lower-back pain or even more troubling financial fears. The devastation of passing over the barricade of sixty (how could it have happened so quickly?) concerns itself with confronting the sheer reality that you are no longer attractive to younger women, and by younger women, I'm now talking about ages thirty-three to thirty-eight. You can buy their love in some cases, obviously, but if you think they like what happens under the covers, well, sober up, stud muffin. In his novel *Disgrace*, J. M. Coetzee told of how it really is, from the standpoint of the trophy bride.

"She does resist. All she does is avert herself; avert her lips, avert her eyes. Not rape, not quite like that. But undesired nevertheless, undesired to the core. As though she decided to go slack, die within herself during the duration, like a rabbit in the jaws of the fox close to its neck. So that everything done to her might be done, as it were, far away."

I overheard a conversation between two Texas women, flush with the flower of youth, who expressed those feelings not quite as artistically but still just as brutally harsh. "These old guys that come on to me—they all have this old-man smell to them. It makes me sick."

"What kind of smell?"

"Oh, I dunno. Like furniture polish."

Now a fellow like Jerry Jones, a man with a ferocious sense of dignity and pride that exceeds the bounds of most, he'll try to fight back. Like all of us Bomber Boomers, especially the ones who partied too heavily in our long-past prime, he gazed into a mirror and observed a face that looked, as they say in Arkansas, like a mud fence after a hard day's rain. Plus, that flat-bellied guard who played for Frank Broyles's early-1960s Arkansas Razorbacks, the leanest and meanest sons o' bitches that ever put on jockey straps, that guy was finally developing a gut not unlike Nate Newton's. For persons of a narcissistic bent like Jerry, that reality is made even crueller by living in a city like Dallas, with all of its reflective surfaces.

At some point in Jerry Jones's mind, probably sometime between the two seasons of his Chan Gailey administration (1998–1999), Jones embarked upon an almost savage self-reconstruction project. He quit drinking, the direst admission of defeat short of suicide that the ex–party boy will ever undertake. Jerry lost a ton of weight, but when that happens, the bagginess and sagginess that appear in the mirror each morning grow more profound.

Never a man to quit, Jerry chose the ultimate alternative. The face-lift. In fact, he and his wife, Gene, decided to have it done together. Gene's went nicely—but Jerry's, well . . .

According to the propaganda put forth by the cosmetic surgeons, Jones should have been a poster boy for such a procedure. Their literature states, "[T]he best candidate for a face-lift is a man or woman whose face and neck have begun to sag but whose skin still has some elasticity and whose bone structure is strong and well-defined." Hell, that's Jerry, all right.

They try to describe the operation to make it sound easygoing enough, but in some cases, a frontal lobotomy might be more fun. Here's what Jerry underwent: "Incisions begin above the hairline, at the temples, extend in a natural line in front of the ear, or just inside the cartilage at the front of the ear, and continue behind the earlobe to the lower scalp. If the neck needs work, a small incision may also be made under the chin. In general, the surgeon separates the skin from the fat and muscle below. Fat may be trimmed or suctioned from around the neck and chin to improve the contour. The surgeon then tightens the skin and the underlying muscle and membrane, pulls the skin back, and removes the excess. Stitches secure the layers of tissue and close the incisions; staples may be used on the scalp."

Sound like fun? It gets worse. That's when they remove the bandages and present the mirror. We've all seen that scene in the movies. The best ones were enacted by Jack Nicholson, as the Joker in *Batman,* and Vincent Price, when his man-to-bug evolution reached its final phase in *The Fly.*

ARRRGGGGHHHHH!!!!!

And in the case of the face-lift, technically known as the rhytidectomy, that's what happens with the ones that work. A woman once described to me what she had seen: "My face was swollen and bruised like somebody had beaten me up with a baseball bat, and this yellow stuff was oozing out through the stitches. I'll *never* do that again, and anybody who's ever seen what it's really like wouldn't do it the first time."

The doctors will talk about certain post-op complications, such as, "At the beginning, you may look and feel rather strange . . . Your face and neck features may be distorted from the swelling . . . You'll probably be self-conscious about your scars . . . Men find they have to shave in new places—behind the neck and ears—where areas of beard-growing skin have been re-positioned . . . It's not surprising that some patients are disappointed and depressed at first . . ."

So welcome to the post-op world of Jerry Jones. A Dallas dermatologist pointed out that Jerry "might have done too much at once. He lost all that weight, had his teeth fixed, and then, with the surgery, all those changes were a little extreme."

For two years afterward, persons who encountered Jones on the street were inclined to gasp. J. Pierpont Morgan, the quadrillionaire, was grotesquely afflicted with a bulbous growth on his nose. Late in life, he would comment, "Everybody stared at it, but nobody ever said a damn thing."

Thus it was with Jerry. With the passage of time, Jones's face would eventually grow into the reconstruction, and photographed from the correct angle, he looks, well, okay.

But for a man who's been through such an ordeal, the last thing he'll do is hire a man like Bill Parcells and then try to pick a fight.

★   ★   ★

Word that Parcells was indeed en route to Dallas was met with a variety of responses.

I was actually shopping in a store that sells bottled spirits, a genteel place with stylish customers and a staff of what they call friendly and helpful sales professionals, when I heard a conversation between a well-tailored woman buying two quarts of Bombay and the gentleman behind the counter. They were talking current events in Dallas that involved football. I knew that because I heard the man at the counter mention the words "Bill Parcells."

And then I heard the woman say, "Well, I don't like the bastard, because the first thing he'll do is get rid of Emmitt Smith."

Their talk continued in hushed words that I could not overhear at first, but it was obvious that the discussion was gaining intensity, until the sales professional shouted, "Don't you tell me I'm stupid just because I work in a liquor store!"

To which the woman responded, "That's not why you're stupid! You're stupid because you're not from Texas!"

As I drove away, the woman was on the sidewalk, shouting invective at the counterman through the closed glass door. This happened in patrician Highland Park, where voices are never raised.

Such was the emotional impact of the Tuna arriving in Texas.

A man who is afflicted with a gambling disorder—a man who, in fact, lost a bundle on the post–1985 season Super Bowl when he bet that Refrigerator Perry would not score a touchdown, against 100 to 1 odds—had a more benign approach to Parcells's arrival in Dallas. Like many gamblers, he didn't know football but was obsessed with attempting to combat the odds. "I really didn't start watching Parcells until he was coaching that green team [the Jets]," the fellow said. "He's not like most of these coaches, who always do something at the end of the game and fuck up the spread. When the outcome is on the line, Parcells never does anything stupid. Not like Tom Landry. He was the very worst. You're betting on his team, favored by seven and a half, and they're up by seven, two minutes to play, on the other team's one-foot line. Landry would let the clock run out, every damn time. I think it was some Christian thing of his. He'd just do that to punish the gamblers."

The Tuna's official arrival in Dallas was naturally consummated with the great America's Team press conference, staged in the media auditorium at Valley Ranch. The place was jammed, with Jones and Parcells on public display together for the first time. Parcells appeared rather stunned, the reality of the situation just now sinking in. Jerry wanted to smile but could not, because his face was evidently still too stiff, even after the removal of the stitches and staples. Yet, it was the glow behind the eyes that now transcended any apparent disfigurement of the cheek and jaw.

The two of them sat on the platform like an old married couple, too brittle for tango lessons but not yet blind enough for assisted living.

The first media question came from a talking head of hair who works for the local market Fox-Southwest cable channel. "S-o-o-o-o-o, Bill. Why do they call you the Tuna?"

That was the dumbest question to be issued from the annals of Texas sports media since the press conference that immediately followed Mickey Mantle's liver transplant operation, when some sportswritin' fool asked the surgeon, "Can you tell us the condition of the donor?"

Poor Tuna. In the old days, back on the East Coast, he might have reenacted the moment when, after an unfortunate reporter asked an even more unfortunate question, Parcells had retorted, "Aw, gimme a break with that stupid dumb-ass question. That's a dumb-ass question. That's a dumb-ass question. You gimme a break with that crap. Aw, you don't know what you're talking about. You're a jerk."

That was the old Tuna. Now here was the new, over-sixty Tuna, starting a new life in a new world. All he could do was gape at the reporter and wonder what in the fuck he had gotten himself into.

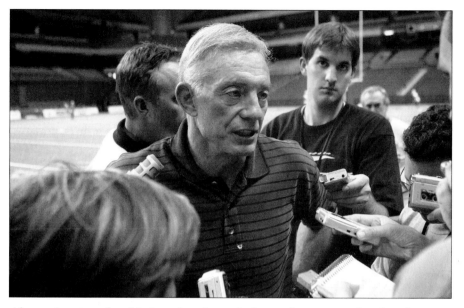

After undergoing a face-lift, Jerry Jones's new look was often compared to that of a movie star, most notably Vincent Price in *The Fly*.

Forever befuddled as Dallas's head coach (2000–2002), Dave Campo's combined 15–33 record became a prime example of what happens when Murphy's Law collides with the Peter Principle.

For over a decade, Joe Avezzano established himself as a fan favorite as the Cowboys' special teams coach. But his tenure with the Cowboys ended when Bill Parcells arrived in Texas, and there was no doubt that Coach Joe was gone for good after the Tuna made a surprise call to a sports-talk radio show.

NFL insiders were stunned when Bill Parcells, the autocrat, went to work for Jerry Jones, the ultimate micromanager. The experts were even more shocked when the happy couple, shown here, engaged in a football version of a storybook romance.

After Emmitt Smith trashtalked his former Dallas teammates, literally, in a *Sports Illustrated* interview, one former player predicted that the Cowboys would "tear his fucking head off" when they faced Smith in the regular season. They didn't tear his fucking head off, as it turned out, but they did break his fucking shoulder.

Chad Hutchinson, the man who'd reigned as the people's choice to quarterback the 2003 Cowboys, incurred the Tuna's displeasure during pre-season play. Hutchinson was banished to the bench, and later all the way to NFL Europe.

Derek Ross was tabbed as a cornerback with a future after his rookie season in 2002. Under Parcells, Ross's future was in the unemployment line after he failed to show up for an appearance at a children's hospital following the Miami game.

Parcells—the Jock Whisperer—attempts to explain the meaning of life to Antonio Bryant. The wide receiver had been regarded as one of the unruliest inmates in the 2002 Cowboys' asylum under the previous coach, Dave Campo.

Nobody is exempt from the wrath of the Tuna, including veteran linebacker Dexter Coakley.

Larry Allen spent so much of the pre-season off the practice field and on the exercise bike that Parcells offered him a yellow Tour de France jersey. The Jock Whisperer inside Parcells told him that there was still something left of Allen the football player who could and would go jaw to jaw with a few more defensive tackles and fuck 'em up good, just for old times' sake.

When Terry Glenn was playing for the New England Patriots, Parcells once referred to him as "she." But as a Dallas Cowboy, Glenn responded with big catches throughout the season.

A dominant defensive lineman was at the top of Parcells's wish list in the 2003 draft. Instead, Dallas selected cornerback Terrence Newman, who proved to be the potential second coming of Deion Sanders.

Under the guidance of Bill Parcells and his staff, quarterback Quincy Carter—regarded by his vast legion of critics as a scatter-armed washout—emerged as the man who would lead the Cowboys' astonishing march to the playoffs.

Offensive tackle Flozell Adams became the Jock Whisperer's prime success story in 2003. Adams not only made the Pro Bowl roster, but also established himself as a future member of the Weight Watchers Hall of Fame.

As an ESPN analyst, Bill Parcells labeled Roy Williams "a young Ronnie Lott." The Tuna wouldn't be disappointed as Williams's coach when the defensive back made teeth-rattling hits like this one against the Philadelphia Eagles.

Darren Woodson not only provided veteran stability to the Dallas defense, he established himself on the NFL's most-wanted list for helmet-to-helmet hitting infractions.

Rookie tight end Jason Witten moves upfield after a pass reception. One of Parcells's favorites, the Tuna encouraged Witten to lead a team cheer after he'd broken his jaw against Arizona.

Parcells summed up Year One of his Texas experience: "As far as an anxiety-provoking season, it wasn't that bad, really, as I look back on it. You know how sometimes you wake up in the middle of the night, like two or three in the morning, and you're sort of over-come with this awful feeling of dread, and you throw up in your mouth? That didn't hap-pen very much, not this year."

CHAPTER 7

OUT WITH THE OLD REGIME AND IN WITH THE NEW

For fifteen years, Randy Galloway's *Sports at Six* ruled North Texas afternoon drive-time radio. Galloway's day job was writing a sports column for *The Dallas Morning News,* but the radio gig became his skyrocket to celebrity.

As the concept of sports talk radio emerged in the mid-1970s and then expanded and prospered, stations liked to use local sportswriters as call-in hosts. This was done for two reasons. First, the sportswriters were knowledgeable. They knew their topics and the personalities involved better than anybody else in town. And second, they'd work for twenty bucks a show and a box of popcorn.

Sometimes, the personality of the writer would present something extra, and voilà, a star is born. That's how people like

Edward R. Murrow and Walter Cronkite—ex–newspaper guys—got their start. Cronkite, in fact, made his debut as a broadcast personality when he became a play-by-play voice for a station that carried Oklahoma Sooners football games.

Galloway's ticket to riches was expedited by the station he worked for—WBAP 820, a self-described "50,000-watt blow-torch" that put out a signal that could be heard in Guam if the weather was right. Additionally, his ratings were greatly enhanced by his lead-in, Paul Harvey's *The Rest of the Story*, the little ironic vignettes with the wry twists at the conclusion that warm hearts throughout the land—"and little could anyone have guessed that the heroic little Chuckie, who bravely landed the 747 after the pilot had dropped dead of a heart attack, that little Chuckie was . . . a blind cocker spaniel. And now *you* know the r-e-s-s-s-t of the story."

Okay, so maybe Paul Harvey provided the initial audience for the sports program that immediately followed, but it was up to Galloway to keep it. He accomplished that with a native Texan voice—Galloway carried the authoritative tone of a wrecker driver, a rolling, down-home Lone Star accent, the deep drawl that is heard on radio commercials for products like canned chili and toolboxes.

Nor should one overlook the fact that anybody named Randy cannot help but succeed in Texas. Randy is a much-honored name in these parts, and there are more Randys in Texas than there are Joses in Mexico. Now, there are probably more newspaper sportswriters in Texas who can recite the complete works of Ralph Waldo Emerson than there are those who could qualify as financially well-to-do. Not Galloway, who takes his wife on cruises along the Riviera and belongs to a group of investors who own some gently used Thoroughbreds of the $8,000 claiming race ilk.

Galloway's vast core of listeners could scarcely have realized that the host campaigned for George McGovern against Richard Nixon in 1972.

None of that mattered, of course, when Galloway enjoyed the sports-talk coup of the year in January 1994. Jimmy Johnson, who had been equipped with the hot-line number to get into the program, called Galloway's show and not just predicted, live and on the air, but guaranteed that the Dallas Cowboys would beat San Francisco that coming Sunday in the NFC championship game at Texas Stadium. That became a media event of national proportions at the time, what Barry Switzer would later refer to as "Jimmy's famous six-Heineken phone call."

Fast-forward nine years. Galloway had just finished interviewing his guest, Joe Avezzano, known locally as Coach Joe. He was a popular special-teams coach with the Cowboys and had held that job since Johnson had come to town in 1989. Coach Joe liked to sing and play the guitar on locally aired pickup-truck commercials, and he was the darling of the director in the TV production truck at the Cowboys' telecasts.

His Cowboys special teams, as the Johnson era was roaring into Super Bowl prominence, presented a rare élan. Their trademark was Kenneth Gant and his pre-kickoff Shark Dance that sent the fan-arousal quotient all the way through the hole in the Texas Stadium roof. Those were the days. Everybody in town adored Coach Joe, and wherever he ventured, his drinks were always on the house.

During the tenures of Chan Gailey and Dave Campo, Coach Joe became a magnet for the sideline closeup because of his enthusiastically animated expressions and his retro horror-movie hairstyle that was so reminiscent of Lon Chaney's portrayal of Wolfman round midnight when the moon was full.

Perhaps this was to be his undoing. Avezzano was perceived as Dave Campo's co-coach, and as the new Bill Parcells era rolled into town with the fanfare of a Ringling Brothers circus parade, anything visibly connected with the old regime needed to be out the door and gone.

Now Coach Joe was stuck with nothing more than what had been a moonlighting situation, his position as head coach of the Cowboys' Arena League entry, the Dallas Desperados. And working as a head coach in the Arena League ranks as the equivalent of being the emcee in a vaudeville act—"Okay, let's all give a nice, warm Hackensack welcome to Miss Chinkie Grimes, folks! Now take it off, baby! Take it all off!"

So Coach Joe had been invited to talk on the radio airwaves with Randy Galloway, discussing his exclusion from the new staff that Parcells had been assembling. Avezzano seemed to insinuate that the Tuna had been less than up front with him during the hiring process, that he'd been strung along for a couple of weeks before the Tuna cut the string.

After Avezzano's interview, Galloway switched back to his usual format that involved bewailing the wretchedness known as the Texas Rangers baseball team and chatting it up in CB radio style with all his good buddies, the Pep Boys set—Buster from Grand Prairie and Kenny from Kennedale.

And then there was Bill from Irving. Parcells—the Tuna himself—was on the line and desiring to speak with Host Randy. Unlike Jimmy Johnson, Parcells did not have a hot-line to jump onto the program. He'd dialed the regular number, just like Joe Twelvepack and the rest of the boys at the bus station.

Parcells, in his estimation, felt that Joe Avezzano had accused him of being untruthful right there on the electric radio, and the Tuna wanted to set the record straight, then and there. He explained that he'd had to wait that couple of weeks to confirm the availability of his first preference for the special-teams coach, Booby Blah. Parcells said that if Avezzano thought that he had been left unfairly dangling during that interim, it was Coach Joe's misunderstanding, not Coach Parcells's.

So the Galloway program presented yet another rare moment for the radio listener, a call-in from the head coach, and this time, the coach sounded sober. That Bill Parcells made the call established two facets about this man at Valley Ranch with crystal clarity: This guy from the Jersey Shore didn't take kindly to being called a liar, and he did not have his radio dial set on KKDA 770, locally known as the Black Rocker. And from those two truths, a third would emerge. Big Bill don't take no crap off nobody.

The station whose airways the Tuna, brimming with temerity, had just intruded used to fill the late-night hours with country hits, songs like Porter Waggoner's famous "Satisfied Mind." That one included some sage and sad lyrics that went "money can't buy back your youth when you're old . . . a friend when you're lonely, or a love that's grown cold."

Well, the Tuna, on the night that he called the Galloway program, didn't give a flying fuck about youth, friends, or some chilly ex-lover who had changed the locks. What money *can* buy is a staff of assistants that makes the difference between restoring an

NFL franchise to a winning profile or one that slowly sinks back into the murky swirl of pedestrian vulgarity.

At the expense of Joe Avezzano's pride (his paycheck was not necessarily an issue, since he had plenty left on his contract whether he worked or not), Parcells had filled out his retinue of Cowboys assistants with the man he wanted the most. Bruce DeHaven would coach the Dallas special teams in 2003.

In Parcells's estimation, special teams become the ultimate determinant in which coach gets the Gatorade bath at the end of the big game and which one makes the death-row trudge across the field to shake hands with the winner, while offering a fake smile.

Like, perhaps, the thin congratulatory look on George Seifert's face when he approached Parcells on January 20, 1991, in San Francisco. That was at the conclusion of a football game that Bill Parcells, on his deathbed, will remember as the all-time most fulfilling event in his coaching career. The Tuna would refer to that game frequently during his initial voyage with the Cowboys—that NFC championship game between the New York Giants and the San Francisco 49ers. While Parcells has never publicly said so, he cannot understand why that particular game is not framed as the one greatest pro football game ever played. His fondness for that event is energized, of course, because his Giants won. Yet Parcells's emotional attachment to that one particular game—now forever welded into his memory bank—is based entirely on how the victory was accomplished. And it was the Giants' special teams and their place kicker who carried the day.

Parcells had taken his Giants team into San Francisco and the stadium known as Candlestick. The playing surface there was the worst excuse for a gridiron facility in the modern world, making the sands of Iwo Jima seem like the eighteenth fairway at the Augusta National Golf Course. A watered-down and soggy moonscape was what it was, and before any team could overcome Joe Montana, Jerry Rice, Roger Craig, and the remainder of the 49ers' empirically splendid football team, the visitor would first have to overcome the mental blockade that the Candlestick playing field itself imposed, and nobody ever did.

Montana's almighty 'Niners had won back-to-back Super Bowl titles, and no right-minded football theorist could put forward a sane argument that the 1990 regular-season 'Niners were not poised to tack on an unprecedented third.

Parcells's Giants, with their proud linebacker corps of Lawrence Taylor, Gary Reasons, and Carl Banks, sparred well enough against the 49ers in the first half. They'd limited Montana and his West Coast–offense accomplices to two field goals by Mike Cofer. Matt Bahr tacked on two of his own for the Giants, and the game was deadlocked 6–6 at halftime.

In the third quarter, nature returned to its natural course. Montana fired one of his trademark, sudden-strike TDs, this one a sixty-one-yarder to John Taylor. Candlestick Park began to shudder and tremble beneath the reaction of the fans, just as the stadium had done in the late-afternoon hours about a year and a half earlier when the earthquake occurred just prior to game three of the 1989 World Series. Here's a little-known fact about those 49ers fans: For a city that deems itself the paradigm of North American cultural refinement, the individuals who purchase tickets to San Francisco home games are *the* most rabid, vicious, and hostile to fans wearing the colors of the visiting teams in the whole spectrum of the NFL.

Citizens of the Bay Area might take umbrage at such a claim, coming from a native of that barbaric slice of life that constitutes Texas. So how can a person who is the product of terrain rougher than the sex in a Turkish prison come forward with such an assertion? Because at the end of the Cowboys-49ers championship game in 1970 at Kezar Stadium, as I was innocently trudging to the 49ers' dressing room to ask that prick John Brodie how he managed to louse up the game for San Francisco, I got hit in the back of the neck with a full beer bottle, heaved down from somewhere in the stands.

Then a San Francisco cop came to chastise me for straying too far from the chicken wire that separates the normal people from the lunatics who attend the games. Remember, please, that the ancestors of the original 49ers are simply the offspring of cannibals, as anybody familiar with the tale of Donner Pass realizes. Raiders fans? They're imposters—concert violinists dressed like Hell's Angels on a weekend outing. Eagles fans in the Old Vet? With all due respect, they're an Amish picnic compared with the 'Niners' faithful, which is why it is easier to split an atom with a Gillette razor blade than it is to come from behind in the second half in a championship game played in San Francisco.

So that Montana-to-Taylor bolt put the 'Niners ahead, 13–6, and all of the annals of recent history told the world that the Giants were cooked.

Still, New York refused to go away quickly. Bahr connected on a forty-six-yarder to cut the margin to 13–9 by the end of the third quarter. Had this game been played at the Meadowlands, the issue might still have been in doubt. Unfortunately for the Tuna and his group, this was still in the crud and mud of the Bay Area.

Then, as the clock began to drain the hopes and dreams from

the Giants' cause, providence, in the form of 270 pounds' worth of guided muscle named Leonard Marshall, would intervene on New York's behalf. Marshall—Parcells's best defensive lineman—slammed into Montana just as Golden Joe was about to lead one of his patented fourth-quarter drives to put the game away. Montana fumbled the ball.

The 49ers recovered, but Montana did not. The CBS cameras provided a brief close-up of Montana, dazed and on his knees, with a big chunk of that Candlestick Park sod jammed into his helmet's face guard. After countless game-winning collaborations with Jerry Rice and friends, Montana was a beaten man. Football's unbeatable man, on that one key blast by Leonard Marshall, had been transformed into Roberto Duran looking at Sugar Ray Leonard and pleading, *"No mas."* At that precise moment, the NFL's mightiest oak had been felled. After that one play, Joe Montana would not be the same quarterback. Never again. The Giants, with Montana reeling on the sideline, now sensed that the 49ers were no longer unbeatable, but New York's special teams had to seal the deal, if the deal was to be done at all.

The 49ers, not necessarily prone to quit either, stopped the Giants just on the San Francisco side of midfield. Then the Giants sprang a fake punt, with Gary Reasons taking the snap and racing downfield thirty yards. "We'd been studying the 49ers' punt coverage a couple of times and told Gary to call the fake, if he felt it was there. Fortunately for us, it was there," Parcells would say later. Given the eventual outcome, that fake punt would be the play of the game.

The 49ers, tenacious to the end, held on to the lead, but Bahr's fourth field goal cut the margin to 13–12. Still, the angst in the stands, not to mention on the San Francisco team, was running even deeper than the slop between the Candlestick hash marks. When the Giants' Erik Howard stripped the ball from Roger Craig with 2:26 to play, the clattering of rosary beads could be heard over the roar of the surf on both American coasts.

Jeff Hostetler, subbing for the wounded Phil Simms, had not enjoyed what would be remembered as one of the memorable quarterbacking efforts in a championship game. The fact was that Hostetler was not at all fond of his coach, a man well known for browbeating his stars—and his quarterbacks in particular. Parcells didn't care what Hostetler thought. "Hell, all he had to do was play quarterback," the Tuna would remark retrospectively.

When it mattered most, Hostetler came through on two critical plays. The first was a nineteen-yard completion to the tight end, Mark Bavaro, and then came a thirteen-yarder to wide out Steven Baker. Now, with six seconds left, Matt Bahr returned to the field. His forty-two-yarder was no gimme, but the football sailed through the uprights, and the Giants had won, 15–13. It was the kind of football game that Bill Parcells loves best. His team had won on the road in what was then the league's most hostile environment for visitors, his Giants had defeated a team with a roster replete with Hall of Famers, and the Tuna had won the biggest game of his career without scoring a touchdown. "Not the most exciting game in the world, if you judge by the final score, but I'll bet Woody Hayes and Bear Bryant would have enjoyed it" was the Tuna's analysis.

Keena Turner, one of the 49ers' great defensive players, having just been denied a sure shot at a third straight Super Bowl title, viewed the outcome from a different perspective. "Had we won, historically, that would have put us in a different place," Turner said.

Another special-teams event, one that would happen one week to the day later, is better remembered than anything that happened in that Giants-49ers epic. Its place in pro football history is so well embossed, naturally, because it happened in the Super Bowl game.

On the game's climatic play, Buffalo Bills' Scott Norwood missed the forty-seven-yard field goal that would have made the Bills 22–20 winners instead of 20–19 losers. Wide right, by an eyelash, and the tears in Buffalo have not really subsided since. How close was Norwood's kick? Had the ball been placed at the forty-four-yard line, just three lousy yards closer, it would have been good.

Since Parcells would be undergoing heart bypass surgery in the aftermath of those games and would never coach the New York Giants again, it might not have been an act of wisdom to argue the importance of special teams to the Tuna. Parcells might have been thinking of yet another Super Bowl special-teams highlight when he hired Bruce DeHaven to coach that aspect of his new team, the Cowboys.

In his final game when he was head coach of the New England Patriots, in Super Bowl XXXI in New Orleans against the Green Bay Packers, Parcells's underdog Pats were rallying from behind and had just scored a touchdown to cut the Packs' lead to 27–21. The smoke was still thick in the New Orleans Superdome after a halftime extravaganza that featured the Blues Brothers and then a star turn by James Brown singing "I Feel Good," and the Patriots had snared the momentum.

That momentum would last through about three minutes' worth of high-dollar Super Bowl commercials. When the cameras returned to New Orleans, Desmond Howard of the Packers took the next kickoff and went ninety-nine yards, ensuring a Packers victory and providing the wives of every household in Wisconsin a reprieve from what surely would have been remembered as the most abusive winter in the history of the state.

What Bill Parcells remembers—and it's the littlest of details that remain branded in this man's amazing sense of recall—about *that* play was that an injury-mandated substitute was playing third man from left, outside on the Patriots' kickoff coverage unit, and it was that player's breakdown that enabled Desmond Howard to take the return all the way back.

With Bruce DeHaven coaching his special teams, calamities like that might not happen on a distant Sunday afternoon when Bill Parcells, coaching the Dallas Cowboys, could face a crucial moment in a Super Bowl game. The Tuna plans his minutiae years in advance.

Parcells had been admiring the work of DeHaven from afar for the better part of a decade and a half. Simply stated, DeHaven was the Tuna's kind of guy. DeHaven had graduated from Southwestern, which evidently is a college in Kansas. Parcells, himself a graduate of Wichita State, is clearly partial to these guys from the Sunflower State.

Shit, that's where all that *In Cold Blood* stuff took place. Man, they grow 'em up mean in Kansas. And, like the Tuna himself, DeHaven had made more obscure career stopovers than an Irish gypsy. These included assignments with the Pittsburgh Maulers and Orlando Renegades of the whatever-the-hell they used to have before NASCAR got big.

Parcells had hired DeHaven away from the 49ers, where he'd been in charge of the special teams in 2000, 2001, and 2002. As a commentator with ESPN, the Tuna realized that Vinny Sutherland and Jimmy Williams had enjoyed big-time seasons under DeHaven's direction.

But here's what intrigued Parcells most about Bruce De-Haven. Prior to joining the 49ers, DeHaven had coached the special teams with the Buffalo Bills. What that meant was that DeHaven had tutored the player who would rank as the greatest special-teams coverage man ever to play the game—Steve Tasker.

When it comes to the category of "hidden" or "invisible" yardage—in other words, the stats that the fan doesn't read in his Monday sports section—the guys like Steve Tasker are the people who provide those so-called hidden yards.

Steve Tasker—all five feet nine and 181 pounds of him—participated in 195 NFL regular-season and playoff games and was credited with 204 tackles and 7 blocked punts. Parcells joked that when he was competing against him, he'd begged Steve Tasker to retire on several occasions. How many special-teams players are awarded the MVP in the Pro Bowl? Well, one guy did it, and that was Tasker. So what if Tasker had been kicked out of the final game of his playing career, when he decided to collide with a game official instead of the man carrying the football. Yeah, Tasker had played collegiately at Northwestern, which is known for producing people whose life intention is to become rich. But he'd grown up in Kansas.

Bill Parcells realized that they don't make guys like Steve Tasker anymore. With that in mind, the Tuna told Bruce DeHaven to go out and find him one anyway. While the courts might deny me the right to examine the contract that Bruce DeHaven signed with the Dallas Cowboys under Bill Parcells's terms, I'll bet that there is a provision somewhere right at the top that reads "Get your ass over to Kansas and find me a natural-born special-teams killer."

If the presence of Bruce DeHaven brought comfort to the psyche of the Tuna as he approached the monumental project of retooling what had become, from a comedy standpoint, America's Scream, that would not outweigh the hiring of another Parcells favorite, Maurice Carthon.

Technically, Carthon's title would be that of offensive coordinator, an assignation that carried a recent curse from the standpoint of the Dallas Cowboys. Bruce Coslet, who had attempted to install a West Coast offense with Mosquito Coast talent, lasted one miserable season in 2002. Coslet had replaced the unfortunate Jack Riley, who had overseen the final years of Troy Aikman's disintegration and Dallas's well-founded reputation for shooting blanks when the Cowboys had the ball.

Carthon, in actuality, would not serve the traditional role of the modern offensive coordinator—initiating attack plans, designing schemes, or even calling the plays. Carthon's role would be more of a practice-field-technique coach and, more important, a special instructor in the category of attitude.

Like so many of Parcells's favorites, Carthon was a product of the sticks. He grew up in Oseola, Arkansas, a community that is probably best known as the former place of residence of Albert King, a Mississippi blues titan of the scratchy old 78-rpm era. Carthon's hometown is also—if not the actual birthplace—

vaguely connected with the creation of two songs: "Lumpy Dumpy, You Big Fat Ape" and "Go Dance with the Fat Girl."

Carthon's reputation, when he came out of Arkansas State with the intention of earning a living playing professional football, was hardly synonymous with names like Hershel Walker. But Walker himself would learn of Carthon soon enough. When Hershel was making his first large dollars with the New Jersey Generals of that old W league, Maurice Carthon, the fullback, was Walker's lead blocker. Some sportswriter attached the word "punishing" to Carthon's playing style, and nobody, Bill Parcells included, would ever see any reason to amend that description.

Big Bill and Carthon would first cross paths with the Giants in 1985, the year that Parcells would prove to himself that he could function as a head coach in the NFL while somehow avoiding hospitalization in a place where the patients get to play with modeling clay all day long. In the Tuna's offensive scheme that featured ten-ton trucks as running backs, Carthon served as the battering ram. Joe Morris, Ottis Anderson, and Rodney Hampton all owe large portions of their yardage stats, not to mention their professional reputations, to Carthon's ferocious and relentless trail guidance into the mean and bloody trenches.

Carthon's playing career extended through 1992. Working at a position that was not conducive to longevity, he never missed a game due to injury. There is an age-old story about the football coach from the leather-helmet era who allegedly commented, "My fullback does not know the meaning of the word 'fear.' Of course, he doesn't know the meaning of a lot of other words, either."

This would not apply to Maurice Carthon. Since ending his playing career, Carthon has emerged as one of professional football's most astute operatives in installing a running game. If Parcells is the Jock Whisperer when it comes to the individual motivation of the fifty-three moving parts of a pro football roster, Carthon maintains a rare gift when it comes to penetrating the mind-set of the running back.

Curtis Martin, it must be remembered, was merely a third-round draft choice out of Pitt when he joined the New England Patriots in 1995. Under Carthon's direction, Martin ran for 1,487 rookie yards, scored fourteen touchdowns, and promptly sealed his identity as one of the premier hit-the-hole and make-the-daylight-whether-it's-there-or-not virtuosos of the whole league.

After moving over to the Jets, Carthon produced running backs who produced a thousand yards or better for four consecutive seasons. That is significant only in the context that, prior to Carthon's arrival, the Jets had produced a one-thousand-yard rusher exactly four times in their thirty-seven seasons.

Darren Woodson, the one player on the Cowboys roster who could be qualified to comment on such a topic (offensive guard Larry Allen would be another, except that Allen has never been known to utter anything beyond a monosyllable in public), watched Parcells and Carthon work together in a minicamp and said, "There's a history between them. Carthon is like Little Bill. Nowadays, players seem to want kinder, gentler coaches, but Bill is not that way and neither is Carthon. His attitude is 'I'm going to get on you and stay on you. I hate losing, and Bill is the same way.' Carthon hates mistakes. And Bill is the same way. He has the same mentality as Bill. They're essentially the same guy."

Yet another huge piece to the Parcells Dallas staff came with the hiring of Sean Payton, recently of the New York Giants. Payton enjoyed an expanding reputation as a master at devising TD-producing strategies within the NFL red zone.

Still, the media deemed Payton as a curious hire. Payton had fallen into disrepute in the media eye, at least. During the 2002 season, Giants head coach Jim Fassel had essentially demoted Payton during a key stretch of the season, removing him from his play-calling duties. After that, the Giants got hot and stormed into the playoffs, before blowing a big lead in a controversial loss at San Francisco.

The Sean Payton who Parcells was bringing to Texas appeared to be damaged goods. Parcells realized otherwise. He had studied Payton's overview of the art of offensive war. Payton had his own role models among the offensive coordinators around the league and had noted, "Each has their own style, but I think what they have in common is they build their packages around their personnel." Given that—if Payton had his druthers from the standpoint of personnel—the one plaything he most desired would be a tight end who was a Sherman tank with soft hands. Those come in handy inside the red zone. Theologically, then, Sean Payton and Bill Parcells had been baptized in the same creek.

The Tuna's new offensive staff took on the look of an odd troika. Who's in charge of the task of injecting some signs of life into this dead horse of a Dallas offense—Carthon, Payton, or the Tuna Man? You know what they say, too many chefs fuck up the soufflé. Not that Parcells appeared to be on the verge of entering counseling in order to ease the angst of the sports talk-show hosts. Parcells's advice to those who are unfamiliar with the arcane workings of his behind-closed-doors coaching operation is and always has been: "Don't worry about it. It's just a group of guys messing around with an odd-shaped ball." Parcells might also have added a line that he likes to use when concerned citizens occasionally question his motives. "Pro football is not a game for well-adjusted people," the Tuna reminds them.

From the defensive aspect, Parcells elected to maintain Dallas's status quo. Mike Zimmer, the defensive coordinator in the Dave Campo asylum, would be allowed to retain his post.

The Mike Zimmer defenses on those 5–11 Campo teams had produced some interestingly impressive stats during those dreadfully inept times. Dallas's NFL ranking in the myriad of categories stood surprisingly respectable, usually placing it in midpack and sometimes Top 10 in surrendering yardage, touchdowns, production of turnovers, etc. To a certain extent, Zimmer's coaching accomplishments on those lost-in-space Cowboys teams were tantamount to accepting a role in *Earth Girls Are Easy* and winning the Oscar for best supporting actor.

It was not necessarily Mike Zimmer's statistical résumé that earned him the job of handling Bill Parcells's defense. Zimmer maintained a variety of intangibles that the Tuna admires in coaches.

Zimmer's high school head coach had been his father. Parcells knows that when it comes to developing a tough hide, no better indoctrination, other than being Mike Tyson's cell mate, comes from playing high school football under your old man, particularly when you're the quarterback.

Zimmer was the product of one of those off-Broadway colleges that the Tuna seems to favor. In this case, it was Illinois State. And it gets better. Zimmer's quarterbacking career ended when he broke a thumb. So they moved him to linebacker, where his playing was ended for good after Zimmer had to undergo neck surgery. Hell, the sumbitch is probably lucky he wasn't stuck in a wheelchair for the rest of his life. Therefore, in the Tuna's estimation, Mike Zimmer is a man who understands the game. Plus, there was never a sideline shot on TV that depicted Mike Zimmer without a grimace on his face, like G.I. Joe charging up the hill with a bazooka in both hands and a bayonet in his teeth.

Oh, one other thing the Tuna admired in Mike Zimmer. During the 2002 season, he developed a tandem at defensive safety—Darren Woodson and Roy Williams—who probably led the league in the production of concussions among opposition players. In fact, any offensive skill-position players in the league who really understood the game were scared shitless of those two.

Bill Parcells had now collected the essential parts to a coaching staff that was endowed with not only a tunnel-vision approach to the game based around the no-excuses concept, but also a group of guys—band of brothers, if you will—that was void of any and all traces of human compassion. So in the monumental project of rejuvenating the Dallas Cowboys, step one was already in place.

Step two would follow shortly, as the Tuna's dictatorial fetishes would become pervasive throughout Valley Ranch. Under the less-disciplined environment of previous regimes, the Cowboys office complex had taken on something of a frat-house, wide-open-door policy. It was a place where a young reporter like Kevin Lyons of the Fort Worth *Star-Telegram,* described by a coworker at the paper as being "about twenty-eight, going on sixteen," could actually storm into the office of Jerry Jones and accuse the owner of lying to him. Then the two would stand toe-to-toe, joyously shouting "Fuck you!" into each other's face.

Now that the Tuna was on the scene, it was good-bye frat house, hello Kremlin. Parcells issued his first abiding executive mandate. From day one, and throughout the regular season, no assistant coaches would be allowed to speak with the media. Any and all comments would come directly from the Tuna. (The regular season would end, and guess what? The assistants wouldn't talk then, either.)

There was talk that new security cameras had been installed throughout Valley Ranch. Big Brother was in charge now. Compared with this setting, the Bush White House was a honky-tonk. In Parcells's view, if confrontation is good for the soul, then paranoia is even better.

CHAPTER 8

TUNA'S TWENTY PERCENTERS

For a man possessed of enough superstition to get elected as the congressional representative from Middle Earth, Bill Parcells had to have been alarmed at the omen that arrived on his doorstep in his first weeks on the job as the new CEO of the Football Division of Dallas Cowboys Industries, Ltd.

Nonwork-related distractions, particularly those of the off-the-field shenanigans variety, reign as the rankest of offenders on Parcells's organizational enemies list.

"The main reason that he [Parcells] brought me down here, I think, was to communicate to the rest of the team that the creation of those so-called distractions are the first thing that will get you a one-way ticket out of here," receiver Terry Glenn told me. (He'd been traded to Dallas from Green Bay.) This was the same Terry Glenn whom Parcells had immortalized as "she" during their days together with the Patriots and the same Terry Glenn who had been identified by an ex-girlfriend as "a man with Pro Bowl talent and a blues singer's life." Glenn, evidently, had grown up a lot since those days, hence the summons from Parcells.

So when cornerback Dwayne Goodrich was arrested in late January 2003 and charged with running over and killing two men who were helping out at a previous accident scene on the LBJ Freeway north of Dallas and then fleeing, how could Parcells not find a disturbing harbinger of coming events? Some witness statements had Goodrich's car going about one hundred miles per hour at the time of the tragedy.

Goodrich, the player who was burned by Terrell Owens in the final seconds of the 2002 49ers game that finalized Dave Campo's passing as Dallas's head coach, would shortly be cut from the roster anyway. But the awfulness of Goodrich's situation simply illustrated the profound nature of the lurking curse that lies beneath the glitz of the star on the Cowboys' helmets.

"I think that star on the helmet was the reason that Dwayne left the scene of the wreck, and that's what so greatly compounded his problems with the law," said a member of his defense team. "It's that star that makes those Cowboys feel so conspicuous—because they *are* conspicuous. And the star, believe me, doesn't bring any special favors with the law in this town, despite what that stupid bitch with the double-digit IQ wrote in the local paper, because it's exactly the other way around. If Goodrich had been some plumber from Garland, he'd have gotten fairer treatment from the DA's office."

The problem with the silver star on the football helmets versus the silver star on the chest of law enforcement exists as one of the downside factors that come from coaching a team that exceeds the lounge-act status in the NFL that Parcells was talking about when he took the job.

Difficulties arising in the realm of public image were magnified when Jerry Jones, during his "slump years" as general manager, brought in a couple of players already known to have insurmountable psychiatric problems. Take, for example, Alonzo "Big Daddy" Spellman, a defensive lineman who would eventually be arrested for some unacceptable behavior on a commercial air flight. Later, a judge would confine Spellman to a mental-health facility, noting that the former Ohio State Buckeye star was "too dangerous to be on the street." That assessment moved a Dallas sports commentator named Dale Hansen to note, "The problem was that Spellman wasn't dangerous *enough* on the football field."

Worse yet was the case of Demitrius Underwood, a defensive end, whose tragic delusions reached the point—and could it get any more extreme for a Dallas Cowboy?—that the afternoon finally came when Underwood thought he was a cop.

Underwood, in fact, was directing traffic at a busy intersection in Irving, when a woman motorist, attempting to turn, assumed that the man in the street was one of the homeless and handed him a $5 bill. That's when Underwood yanked the woman from her vehicle and attempted to arrest her on charges of bribing a law enforcement officer, before being arrested himself. Demitrius Underwood, to his credit, left no remaining ambiguities in the question of whether or not he would qualify as the sort of guy the Tuna likes to have on his roster.

Throughout his extended tenure as a head coach, Parcells has presented his players with a basic guidepost to a peaceful off-the-field existence, an axiom that he says he learned from his father: Avoid places where they don't know you or where you are not welcome. If the Dallas Cowboys players applied the rule, one thing was for sure. They'd be staying away from church.

Parcells was fully aware that the glare of the Cowboys star can present problems beyond the players who wind up in handcuffs. The magnetic effect upon the mass media that the Cowboys' fishbowl syndrome evokes would be his prime adversary in rebuilding the franchise. The Tuna realized that when he came here.

While it would be Jerry Jones's task to expedite Emmitt Smith's departure now that Parcells was in town, there could be no doubt that this issue had been fully discussed and resolved before Big Bill would accept the Dallas job. The erosive effects of advancing age upon Smith's ability to run the football was a secondary factor—if that—in his leaving. Had he stayed, Smith's on-the-field presence would have been diminished, and the daily interrogation that the tsetse flies of the area media would inflict upon both Smith and his coach would be too much for either party to bear. Parcells could clearly see that coming.

As the media influence upon the activities of every big-league sports franchise continues its exponential expansion, the time has clearly arrived that dictates that the stories featured at the top of the hour on the newscasts and above-the-fold headlines involve not what the player did out on the field but what he had to say about it afterward.

Emmitt Smith became a clear example of that early in the 2001 season, his next to last in Dallas. After Quincy Carter, the quarterback personally selected by Jerry Jones in the draft and prematurely hustled into the starting lineup as a rookie, had gotten hurt, his replacement, Anthony Wright, had been less than so-so in a losing effort against the San Diego Chargers, although Wright had thrown a nice ball or two. Afterward, a reporter carrying the only thing deadlier than a loaded rifle—a live microphone—approached Smith and asked a generic question: "Does Anthony Wright deserve to make another start?" He didn't ask when, or in whose uniform, for that matter.

And Smith, out of polite deference to the inexperienced and struggling kid trying his best to function amid the most difficult of possible circumstances, had said, "Yes."

The bloodhounds of the public press provided their own interpretation. They rushed back over to the sad territory occupied by the overmatched coach, Dave "the Fox" Campo, and blared, "Emmitt Smith says that Anthony Wright is better than Quincy Carter, and that Wright is the guy who deserves to be the starter, and that you and Jerry Jones have gravel stuffed inside your heads." Or words to that effect.

Poor Campo. He hadn't heard the innocent "yes" that had been the full extent of Smith's participation in this sudden and home-cooked instant controversy. So Campo could only say, "Somebody needs to tell Emmitt that his job is not to coach this football team."

Aha! A range war that had begun over nothing had gathered full traction, and since the Cowboys were going nowhere as a football team, that cauldron of a nonstory continued to gurgle and boil for half of the remainder of the season. Of all the factors that can poison the water hole for a pro football team, the media igniting little alley fires over nonissues is the last thing a coach should tolerate. "That was one of the things that helped get me over the hump as a coach in this league," Parcells insists. He learned that during his second year with the Giants; thus the sign that is one of the more unusual adornments that you'll see at the Tuna's office at Valley Ranch, the little plaque that reads JUST COACH.

God knows, Parcells had his agenda overloaded already, attempting to locate the players who could play, and the ones who wanted to play, on a roster coming off three straight 5–11 seasons. Parcells had assembled the veterans of that death march and offered a single message. "Raise your expectations [and lose weight]," he'd told them, knowing full well that selling somebody on himself is the hardest selling that it's possible to do. Parcells was still an avid believer in the "80-20" theory that goes with any successful organization, that the 20 percent of the workforce that's the most talented always generates 80 percent of the positive results. With these Cowboys, the task of locating enough players to constitute a reasonable 20 percent might become a brain-blowing task. So the Tuna had no time whatsoever for any horseshit media Ping-Pong matches with a Hall of Fame halfback. So if Emmitt Smith would have to leave and move to Arizona even though he did not have tuberculosis, which is the only logical reason anybody could have to live out there, then so be it.

If Parcells was beginning to question his decision to make his comeback in the Dallas spotlight over the Emmitt Smith controversy, those doubts would deepen shortly enough. No sooner had Emmitt Smith been released than rumors of the second coming of another figure from Dallas's Super Bowl triumvirate of a decade past began to surface. Somebody, somewhere, had planted the seed that Troy Aikman was toying with the notion of a comeback.

How could that make any sense? Aikman, it seemed, had sustained more career concussions than he had TD passes. Aikman's career as one of the league's premier quarterbacks had lingered beyond the 1996 season, but that reputation was bogus. During Barry Switzer's final season in 1997, Aikman played with the intensity of a quarterback who was trying to get his coach fired. That theory was probably ample enough.

Then, in a playoff game against Arizona at Texas Stadium in 1998, Aikman looked as if he were not only trying to get Chan Gailey fired, but also perhaps was trying to entice Jerry Jones to jump off the roof of the Adolphus Hotel in the process. For the remaining two seasons of his career, Aikman, though he could still throw the deep sideline pattern as well as anybody in the history of the position, had become a defensive coordinator's nocturnal emission. The slightest disturbance of his routine within the pocket—and those had become easily accomplished for most defenses as the Cowboys' interior line was in a state of decline—and Aikman was done. Either he would fall to the turf upon first contact or fling the football toward the sideline. Things had become so dreadful that it was all the more understandable that Stephen King ranks as one of Aikman's all-time heroes.

Aikman had developed a postgame quote that he delivered like the canned spiel of a door-to-door guy selling Kirby vacuum cleaners. "They [the other team] made the most of their opportunities and made some big plays. We failed to do that. We had our chances and let them get away." That had become Troy's week-to-week litany, and when Jones cut him loose after the 2000 season ended, even Aikman was probably surprised that no team in the league—not one—was willing to offer him even a minimum salary to see if there might be something left of his talents in a new atmosphere.

And now there was talk that he might come back. This was the product of Aikman, who, according to one of my intrepid sources, "was farting around" and provided an open-ended nonanswer to a reporter's question of whether he might someday entertain the notion of a comeback. So the media, albeit half-heartedly, sprinkled what they regarded as Troy's vague hint into the notes columns. North Texas fans loved that, because Troy Aikman had enjoyed a reign as the most sacred of cows to ever graze in Dallas. Jerry Jones, when asked for a comment, could only shrug and say, "Well, aw shucks, everyone loves Troy and what he did for the franchise, so maybe . . ."

Aikman himself would say, "Ordinarily, of course not, but if a coach of Bill Parcells's stature would *ask* me back, then maybe . . ."

Parcells, on the spot, could only say, "Gee whiz, the guy's one of the all-time greats, so maybe . . ."

What Bill could have said was "He's been locked away in that Fox broadcast booth for two full years now, and I understand what that does to the soul of the competitor." But the Tuna—and he'd been a TV analyst himself during Aikman's final season— had witnessed the wreckage of what was once a dynamic force. Aikman had looked addled and gun-shy. Roger Staubach—hell, maybe Dandy Don—could make it back before Aikman could. More telling than his on-the-field tortures, from Parcells's per-spective, was something that Aikman had said late in his career:

"Losing doesn't eat at me anymore, the way it used to. I get ready for the next play, the next game, the next season."

The Aikman comeback story died soon enough, and its obituary actually appeared on the "motor sports" page of the sports section, not in "Cowboys Notes."

Troy, who formed an alliance with Staubach to own a NASCAR racing team, had mentioned in passing to a reporter attending some promo event at the Texas Motor Speedway that the comeback story was somebody's pipe dream and nothing more. He also denied that Dwayne Goodrich, if he ever got out of jail, would be hired to drive the racecar. Given his "track record" in the criminal courts, Goodrich would have been great on the straightaways but hell on the pit crews.

One less item for the Tuna to worry about.

Now he could return to the confounding task of identifying the 20 percent of the roster that would be providing positive energy, and here he could only hope that the vital plays on coming Sundays would enable the Cowboys to slowly evacuate their crypt and once again terrorize the landscape of the various nearby hamlets of the NFL. Having identified that 20 percent, the Tuna could then begin inflicting his program of sadistic mental conditioning upon the chosen ones. Parcells politely calls this "offering added support to the high achievers." That amounts to jabbing the potential Pro Bowlers with a cattle prod until results appear in the win column. Then the Tuna gives the conquering heroes Sunday night off and begins the entire abusive process again on Monday morning. While Parcells deplores the notion that a word like "abuse" could be applied to his coaching technique—"Mean? Malicious? Nasty? No. No. Never!"—certain players might insist otherwise.

Whatever the interpretation, Parcells had reviewed the on-the-field job performance of his existing roster and identified a handful that would be initial targets for special attention. First were his defensive safeties, Roy Williams and Darren Woodson. The Tuna had already pinpointed Williams in his NFL.com column as the guy who reminded him of the young Ronnie Lott. On the previous Thanksgiving, Parcells had devoted his day to watching his nephew perform in a high school game in New Jersey and later watched on television as Roy Williams made hit after thundering hit against the Redskins and then made a touchdown on an interception near the Washington goal line that ensured one of those oh-so-rare Cowboys victories. Woodson was a relic from Dallas's Super Bowl run and in the "senior" stage of his career had seemed to be enjoying the amusement that came from literal head-to-head confrontations with opposing pass receivers that tended to render the opponent comatose. He had become so accomplished at that skill that the league levied a $50,000 fine on Woodson for a lick he'd planted on a Seattle Seahawks receiver during the 2002 season. A memorandum from the commissioner's office, warning players of the consequences of overindulgence in the art of smash-mouth football and the punitive measures that might be involved, is posted in every locker room in the league. The one that appears on the wall of the Cowboys' dressing room at Valley Ranch has Darren Woodson's photo pasted on it, like a mug shot.

Parcells could rely upon defensive tackle La'Roi Glover, a former New Orleans defensive tackle who signed in Dallas as a free agent prior to the 2002 season, as a player with experience, exceptional skill, and a desire to be on the winning side of the football field. Talking with La'Roi Glover, I would discover, is what it might have been like to talk to, say, Sir Laurence Olivier. Glover speaks with a resonant stage voice and enjoys the use of multi-syllable words. So why, if he likes to win, would Glover sign with a pre-Parcells Dallas team. "I did some research," he explained. "I examined the history of this franchise. What you saw, season in and season out, was a tradition for outstanding defense and an even deeper tradition for stud defensive tackles. Bob Lilly. Randy White. Russell Maryland. And even when the team is in a down pattern, the country remains cognizant of that star on the sides of the helmets."

On the offensive side of the football, Parcells had two immediate targets for admission into his 20 percent club. Both played on the left side of the Cowboys' offensive line, an area that, in the previous season, might have been compared to the Hindenburg explosion. Flozell Adams, the left tackle, had been a player equipped with all of the necessary ingredients that the position demands—and the demands are significant in that the left tackle is responsible for fending off the first wave of incoming defensive missiles that will be thrown at the retreating quarterback whenever the ball is thrown. Adams is a player of gigantic physical size and can combine that facility with the footwork of Gene Kelly. Throughout his career, the killer instinct has been missing from Adams's repertoire, and during the 2002 season, it appeared that he really didn't give a shit anyway. Next to him at guard would be Larry Allen. In the Cowboys' Monday night game against the Giants in 2003, John Madden would claim that Allen was one of two players still active in the game who were the greatest in their positions that the league had ever seen. The other was Jerry Rice. But based on 2002, Allen was more under the hill than over the hill. He'd missed the last half of the season with an ankle injury and wasn't much good on most of the plays he'd been in during the first part of the year. With conditioning a primary concern, Parcells had no clue as to what might be left of Larry Allen.

The quarterback becomes an honorary member of the 20 percent club, no matter who he is or on which team he plays. Parcells knew that before he could locate a quarterback to browbeat on a daily basis, he would first have to anoint the guy with the job. Here, Parcells knew that this task would be what special prosecutors like to call "an ongoing investigation." All the Tuna really knew about Quincy Carter and Chad Hutchinson was that they were playing pro football only after failing in minor-league baseball. So he looked at the bright side. Maybe Cooperstown's loss might someday become Canton's gain.

Dallas had made some free-agent additions during the off-season, and most had a history with the Tuna. Their job was not only to embellish Parcells's 20 percent club but also to school the players in the mysterious ways of the Tuna World that they would soon experience. The aforementioned Terry Glenn arrived via the trade, and the team acquired running back/fullback Richie Anderson and offensive tackle Ryan Young, both former Jets under Parcells. Also, the team signed tight end Dan Campbell, an ex-Giant who had become a favorite of Parcells's new assistant, Sean Payton.

Campbell was a novelty on this squad in that he was one of two native Texans on the whole Cowboys roster. Campbell played high school football at Glen Rose, about forty-five minutes west of Fort Worth, a town noted for being the site of a nuclear power plant called Comanche Peak and also famed for the dinosaur tracks that are imprinted in a nearby riverbed. As a star player, Campbell was somehow left unrecruited by a high school powerhouse that operated just down the highway from Glen Rose, the Stephenville Yellow Jackets.

Campbell was probably better off staying home in Glen Rose. The Stephenville program was about to enter a period of decline during what would have been Campbell's tenure there. A person who allegedly had been supplying a few Stephenville players with their steroids had been killed in an auto accident, and the team was headed south.

Also, the Cowboys signed a linebacker, Alshermond Glendale (Al) Singleton, off the Tampa Bay roster. If nothing else, Singleton could show his teammates what a mint condition Super Bowl ring looked like. Another intriguing selling point on Singleton appears in the Cowboys' media guide—he "enjoys snakes and owns two boa constrictors."

Springtime was looming, and with that, the NFL draft. Parcells and his staff had watched tapes of the Cowboys' previous seasons until their eyeballs had ruptured, and one factor was obvious. If Jeff Robinson's knee had healed properly, the 2003 Cowboys could count on having an adequate deep snapper. Other than that, there was no position on the team, in the estimation of Parcells and his assistants, that did not require an immediate transfusion. Dallas would have the number five overall pick in the draft, as well as the number five in the next three rounds. There was some pretty good ammo available in those slots if the team picked right, and given that positioning, it could ill afford any fuck-ups.

At the pre-draft combine that's conducted at Indianapolis

each year in the Hoosier Dome, many of the better-potential players present their wares and are given the same intensified scrutiny as entries in the Westchester Dog Show or on *American Idol*. (During their physical exams, the NFL combine candidates are X-rayed in nineteen different locations.) They are timed in the forty-yard dash, their bench-press capacities are noted, and they receive style points for turning backflips through a flaming hoop. And as at the Miss America Pageant, their powers of articulation are put on display. Yet many of the veterans of this draft routine think of the combine as window dressing, a largely meaningless waste of an otherwise routine winter weekend. Bill Parcells did not even bother to attend the 2004 event. That's because he and most of the persons who really understand the makeup of what a pro football player is and is not actually comprehend that there is some hidden quality that determines the player's future, which cannot be determined or measured by any of the testing procedures that take place at that combine.

The better talent scouts rely upon a special psychological screening. "Oh, look at this item! When this kid was six years old, he stabbed his aunt to death! Sign him up!" Or, "Check out this guy's rap sheet. He had the balls to rob a Korean grocery store! We can always make room for a dude like that. So what if it takes him a half hour to run the forty? This fucker's got character!"

Whether or not Parcells and company had located any such coveted character studies within the ranks of the available livestock, they weren't telling. Judging by the Tuna's expression as the Saturday carnival got under way, one would doubt it. He looked like somebody who was poised to pass a kidney stone. Jerry Jones sat next to the Tuna. He didn't seem any happier. Draft day for both used to be a fun event. Both Jerry and

Parcells used to like to work the draft like an off-duty car sales-man turned loose with his Christmas bonus at the crap tables of the MGM, moving chips all over the board until sunrise. Trade up! Trade down! Hell, let's live it up while we can. But since this would be Jones and Parcells's initial draft with each other— their first time to do it with each other—they'd decided ahead of time to play it straight. No wheelin', no dealin'. Not this year, anyway.

The TV trucks with dishes on top were lined up in the parking lot outside Valley Ranch, but the images they would beam out would be void of drama.

Everybody knew that Carson Palmer, the quarterback from Southern Cal, would be the first pick. That belonged to Cincin-nati. Since it was ordained that Dallas wasn't going to manipulate itself beyond the fifth slot in either direction, it was all but as-sured that the Cowboys' selection was going to be Terrence New-man, the cornerback from Kansas State. If Parcells had his druthers, the team would have moved up one slot and taken Duane Robertson, a defensive tackle from Kentucky. God awmighty, Parcells had identified this team's most pressing need and that was a player who would demand a double-team on the defensive front. But they stayed put, and the selection was New-man. Parcells was not entirely displeased with this pick for four reasons, and the least of the four had been the scouting report that established Newman as an "explosive shutdown corner with great closing speed."

Parcells also liked the fact that Newman was not lacking for self-confidence. Responding to the complaints of others at that combine in Nap Town that the track on which the forties were run was not conducive to eye-catching clockings, Newman, a Big-

12 hundred-meter dash champ, had said, "Who cares? If you're fast, you're fast." And regarding his assessment of the candidates in the draft, Newman had commented, "It's not up to me who gets picked number one. But if it was, I'd pick me." The confidence factor, the Tuna knew, could be a double-edged sword, but in the one position that remains vulnerable to constant attack, an attitude like Newman's is an essential.

What did intrigue Parcells about Newman was his special instinct to seek out the football in midflight and go catch it. Newman had a rare and unique torque dynamic working for him that enabled him to reach and secure the football before the receiver could. When it came to making the catch, Terrence Newman looked like a Willie Mays natural. And finally, Newman was a product of Kansas State. Bill Snyder, the Wildcats coach, had taken a program that had lingered at the end of the trail, as far as college football was concerned, and somehow produced a Top 10 program that could not and would not tolerate Heisman Trophy candidates, pretty boys and party boys.

Second round—Al Johnson, Wisconsin. A six-three, 305-pound center. His size and footwork were not exceptional, and many scouts thought of Johnson as another garden-variety Big-10 OL. Parcells had seen characteristics that pleased him. Tough, nasty blocker. Viciously attacks opponents. Likes to get to the second level and annihilate linebackers. Parcells had dispatched George Warhop, his new offensive-line coach, up to Madison to provide some specialized test to determine how well Johnson could identify defensive alignments. Warhop was happy with the outcome. Johnson, as it turned out, was a native of Brussels, Wisconsin, which is located on a little-known peninsula called Door County that juts out into Lake Michigan. Door County is known for producing some characters that qualify as odd socks. Johnson, with his narrow-set eyes that give one the impression that he might have encountered more than his share of missing persons in his lifetime, stood out as an individual who, if any newspapers should someday have any reason to inquire, would be described by his neighbors as a loner. Another strong point.

His driving record from his collegiate years suggests that Al used to enjoy a cold one. Hell, another former Wisconsin Badger, Mike Webster, a Pittsburgh Steeler, died young. The media requiems all cited Mike's devotion to the jug, and he was the greatest NFL center—ever.

Third round—Jason Witten, tight end, Tennessee. Here Jones and Parcells would strike the rare mother lode. Witten, an underclassman, came with first-round credentials. But he was available high in the third round largely because this was a draft year when few teams were listing tight ends at the top of their wish lists. Here were Witten's traits that won Parcells's attention: "A former defense lineman, he adjusts well to the errant throw." Given the quarterbacks on the Cowboys' roster, Witten would see plenty of those. "While not particularly fast," one of the Cowboys' scouts had noted, "he has a penchant for sneaking down the field for long gainers in the game's most important moments." Mark Bavaro all over again? The Tuna could dream, couldn't he?

Fourth round—Bradie James, linebacker, LSU. The Russian czar, Peter the Great, used to collect men with glandular irregularities—giants, in other words—and show them off to visiting dignitaries at state dinners as a party treat. Parcells had the notion. He likes to collect big linebackers. "You can't have enough of 'em," he often said, and when the Tuna arrived in Dallas, he didn't have a one.

About two weeks following the draft, the draftees and a handful of other undrafted players who were signed as extreme longshots to make the final roster, but sure-shots to at least serve as cannon fodder during training camp, arrived at Valley Ranch to receive their first indoctrination to pro football and the legendary coach. Rookie Camp. Parcells's staff was on hand for the initial meeting; the Tuna gave his traditional "welcome to the team" address. The newest Cowboys were greeted with the following remarks from Parcells himself, and they went, in part, like this: "Okay, fellas. I'm Bill Parcells. I'd like to welcome you to the Dallas Cowboys. This weekend is an orientation of sorts. This is a time when we try to let you guys know and explain to you to the best of our ability how we do things and what we expect from you. To try to teach you in a short period of time the things we think will assist you in your efforts to make the team. In my experience, those people who accept these ideas succeed. Those who don't accept them have very little chance.

"We're not interested in players who have problems. We want you to put all of the problems you have behind you. I don't need guys who have pregnant girlfriends that are calling them on the phone and all that shit. I am too old for it, and I don't care about it. I want guys who can concentrate on being a football player. I want well-conditioned players at proper weight with good endurance. That's what I'm looking for. Everything you do from here on out is evaluated. Don't try to be inconspicuous, because we're going to look for you. Everything you do is part of the evaluation process. We base our evaluation on a few things.

"First of all, we don't feel responsible as a coaching staff to come to the hotel to wake you up to make sure you're where you're supposed to be. We just need you to be there. And you need to be on time. You don't walk into the meetings a minute late. In pro football, if you're late, you get fined. And it's a lot of money. If you oversleep we'll begin to feel that you're not dependable, and we can't count on you. Maybe you're always in trouble. You've got girl problems, you drink too much, or you use drugs. I have zero tolerance for that stuff, so get the message.

"You need to study. If you do not know, do not sit there and pretend you do. You need to go to your position coach and find out exactly how we want you to do things. If it is still not clear and everybody else around seems like they understand it and you do not, and you are afraid to raise your hand and talk to them, that is stupidity on your part. My coaches and I, all we do is coach. We don't go out, and we don't recruit or talk to alumni groups like your college coaches. We don't do anything but coach professional football games. We are here to win games."

Actually, those remarks were drawn from a transcript of the talk Parcells made to his rookie class of 1999, which was printed in his book, *The Final Season*.

"But that was the same speech he made to us when we got here with the Cowboys, word for word," confirms Jason Witten, the tight end, with whom Parcells would draw some vague comparisons to Mike Ditka near the close of his first season. "I know that because I read his book. And you should have seen the looks on the faces of the rookies who were listening to that speech here in Dallas," Witten told me, near the end of the 2003 season. "I've never seen a wider bunch of eyes in my life."

CHAPTER 9

REMEMBER THE ALAMODOME!

At the beginning of the previous century, as the vitality of jazz and the blues led to the emergence of a genuine, made-only-in-America cultural phenomenon, the axiom went like this: The closer you get to the Mississippi River, the better the music gets.

Parenthetically, in the latter stages of that same century, it became well known throughout the state of Texas that the farther you get from Dallas, the better the people get.

Texas is an enormous place, yet I am confident that I have seen all that there is to see—the Big Thicket deep in the woods of the southeastern part of the state, where a man at the Texaco told me, "Around here, we eat what we shoot. Even if it's the goddamn sheriff." I have attended the Fire Ant Festival, held annually in Marshall, near the Louisiana border. I vacation frequently in Port Aransas, the White Trash Waikiki; I have spent happy hours in El Paso, a city of profound historic significance in that the margarita was invented just across the Rio Grande in Juarez. I have had a supernatural experience on an Easter Sunday morning in New London in the Piney Woods of the east, where the school blew up in 1937, and the presence of the dead seemed overwhelming. I have seen the stars from the McDonald Observatory in Fort Davis, a facility funded from the estate of a rich Texan who mandated the construction of a telescope "so strong that you could view the gates of heaven and see who's inside." I have been to Amarillo, the Versailles of the Panhandle, where I got to interview the Lennon Sisters and later witnessed a minor-league ice hockey team trash a motel bar. I have attended the famed chili cook-off in Terlingua and watched people receive honors for producing culinary concoctions that would kill a hyena. I have performed, very briefly, onstage with the Drifters, while in attendance at their Christmas night performance at a hotel in Galveston. There was an ice storm that night, and my wife and I were the only persons there, although she did not remain for my performance. I have not attended the Rattlesnake Roundup in Sweetwater (you've got to draw the line somewhere) but dined at the Dairy Queen there.

For five decades, I've been drinking from the bottomless well that is known as Texana, and never, on any occasion, have I heard anybody say, "When I retire, I want to move to Dallas."

Texans, on the whole, stand out as a people-friendly bunch, easygoing, laid-back, and local. But they don't like the Dallas-oids. A Church of Christ minister in Abilene told me that his denomination believes that in order to ascend to the Promised Land, as a gesture of atonement, he or she must drive through Dallas during rush hour. Lawyers from all parts of the state speak of Dallas lawyers with unbridled contempt, referring to them as those "motherfucking 214 [the Dallas area code] lawyers."

Of the 254 counties in Texas, Dallas County is the only one that has never produced an oil well. It's never produced anything. No cattle fortunes were made in Dallas. No cotton plantations of note. Nothing remotely connected with the economic forces that have served as the DNA of the Texas mystique. No, Dallas is and always has been occupied by the people who bank and invest the fortunes of the wildcatters and rancher barons, but not by the people who fought the Comanches and the Kiowa, the ones who braved the wilderness so that Big D money changers could get rich off the interest.

So Dallas exists as a land with no soul, where men are married to their stock portfolios but sneak around with blond mistresses who have their feet surgically altered to fit inside their Jimmy Choo shoes.

Situated to the south, however, is a different kind of Texas city. That is San Antonio, which is 280 miles and one entire universe away from the Dallas city limits. And this is where the Bill Parcells era, the real balls-to-the-wall football part of it, at least, would actually begin.

Larry McMurtry, in his recent book entitled simply *Roads*, details his travels on the major interstate arteries of North America. He believes that the stretch of highway that he calls "the 35," which runs from Dallas to San Antonio, then down to the border at Laredo, is the most unbearable stretch of highway that he experienced in all of his travels. He's right. That Dallas–San Antonio run is a root canal of a journey, a terrifying behind-the-wheel experience in which the driver joins in a NASCAR-like, bumper-to-bumper race and all of the drivers, manically changing lanes in search of a better drafting partner, stand as living testimony to the ravishes of cheap drugs. For every hour devoted to braving "the 35," one year is subtracted from the traveler's life.

With the lone exception of Carl's Corner, the truck stop that became a town with its six-foot dancing polyurethane mariachi frogs on the roof, off to the right about forty-five miles down the raceway, there is nothing to see and no place worth stopping. Once the driver, assuming that he isn't crushed beneath an eighteen-wheeler hauling parts to some cheap-labor factory across the Mexican border, achieves the end of the ordeal, it becomes worth it.

San Antonio remains the absolute antithesis of all things Dallas. Its architecture is characterized by Valencian influences of the Moorish era, with gentle curves and sweeping, graceful arches. That's in direct conflict with the Dallas look, all reflective glass and harsh, sharp edges, the sixty-story office towers that sprang from the prairie in the 1960s. Giant Wheaties boxes are what they are.

San Antonio remains a city of elegant plazas lined with stately red oaks. Dallas is a city that bulldozes and then paves public golf courses—all for the betterment and good of the developer boys who want to sling up tight rows of gaudy minimansions. San Antonio has its Mission Trail. Dallas has Harry Hines Boulevard, which has several locations where a person can donate blood or, depending upon the prevailing mood of the vice squad, purchase a blow job alongside the Flea Bag Motel.

In 1880 the ice cream soda was invented in San Antonio. In Dallas the mother of Michael Nesmith of the Monkees invented

Liquid Paper, the product that enables all of the Big 4 accounting firms to cook the books. San Antonio has Tim Duncan. Dallas has Mark Cuban.

But—and this is a substantial but—Dallas has the Cowboys, and San Antonio has a rich guy named Red McCombs who owns an NFL franchise, but it happens to be in Minnesota. So for a month in the summertime, Jerry Jones graciously agreed to loan his team to the Alamo City.

Jones's plan to move the Cowboys' preseason training camp to San Antonio prior to the beginning of the 2002 season was the product of sheer Ozark horse sense. For the previous six years, the Cowboys had trained in Wichita Falls, nestled along the Red River badlands and surrounded by nothing that even slightly passes for or resembles civilization. Wichita Falls is best known as a tornado magnet, where the locals enjoy hitting one another in the face with beer bottles. In 2000 some living legends staged a reunion and called it Hoodstock. At midnight, a couple of the old-timers walked into the middle of a street and finished a fist-fight that had ended in a draw in 1959.

Fascinating folklore, but hardly the kind of thing that attracts national media—or even that strange breed of fan who will pay to watch football practice—to your training camp. So Jones made a deal with the city of San Antonio, where people like to visit. And better yet, he presented the novelty of training the team indoors—the great air-conditioned indoors—at the Alamodome.

Now. About that Alamodome. This is a 430,000-square-foot, clear-span, cable-supported structure that looks like the world's largest Erector set. The city built the place in 1993 as the home of the San Antonio Spurs and the site of an NCAA Final Four.

The notion was that Texas A&M and Texas would stage a couple of home football games there and that eventually the NFL would place a franchise in San Antonio.

The Spurs have moved to a new arena; Jacksonville, Carolina, and Houston have been awarded the NFL expansion franchises; and Red McCombs has shown no inclination whatsoever to transfer his Vikings out of the Metrodome. Texas and Texas A&M saw no reason to move any home games away from Austin or College Station. So with the exception of a third-tier bowl game and some Tejano music concerts, not a hell of a lot goes on in the Alamodome.

This vast arena is now largely occupied by various species of bird life, and I know this for sure because, as I stood on the sideline watching the morning session of one of Bill Parcells's two-a-days, one of them crapped on my head. Also, my legs were sucked dry by the most ravenous mosquitos this side of the Everglades.

Still, this beats the hell out of Wichita Falls. And watching a Bill Parcells–designed football practice, for anybody interested in a no-nonsense, not-one-iota-of-wasted-motion exhibition, this ranks as one of those priceless Visa-card moments. This is a non-bullshit environment. As the players lie on the simulated grass field in neat rows and stretch, Parcells strolls among them, a man in control, although life in San Antonio has been what might be termed hectic. Around town, the Tuna, recognizable as he is, has attained superstar status. At the team hotel—the Marriott, which stands as the keystone to the city's River Walk facility—Parcells is ushered in and out aboard a freight elevator.

The media assembly lines the field on the far sideline. Charlie Waters, the former Cowboys defensive star who had coauthored a book with Cliff Harris, was among them. Waters would do pregame radio commentary. Today, he's talking the demise of Washington coach Rick Neuheisal, fired for his participation in the NCAA March Madness betting pool. "I was so glad to see that prissy motherfucker get the ax." He grinned. Waters, a direct and enthusiastic man, left little room for doubt of his personal evaluation of his former coaching rival. "Rick Neuheisal is a god-damn fucking scumbag. When I was at Oregon and he was at Colorado, he did everything he could to run the score up on us in the Cotton Bowl. After the game, my players had to grab me and hold me back, because I was getting ready to kick the continental dog shit out of him."

Pat Summerall, recently deposed as Fox Network's play-by-play man, stands with folded arms and watches. Few people on earth have studied the game of American professional football more thoroughly, more meticulously than Pat Summerall. He is fascinated by Parcells's coaching technique

"Parcells is a natural teacher, and he reminds me of an assistant coach who was my personal coach when I was kicking for the Giants," said Summerall in that distinctive voice of his, the one that became so unmistakable as John Madden's sidekick and straight man for years with CBS and later Fox. "That coach told me never to practice unless he was watching, because if I was using poor technique, he wouldn't be there to correct it. That coach was a guy named Landry."

"That's well and good," I countered. "But how many years of great teaching will be involved in turning this team around?"

"Not as long as you think," said Summerall, sounding very confident in his conviction. "You'll see a difference right away. And by early to mid-season, a big difference."

The Parcells-led practice sessions in this Alamodome, I'm told (and I'd have to be told, since I wasn't there to watch any of this last year), offer a distinct contrast to the sessions here in 2002, which were conducted more for the benefit of the HBO *Hardknocks* extravaganza.

What is a strange scene, as football practices go, is an absence of raised voices. Parcells's practices are intense, but this is a controlled intensity. All of the trains run on time in Tuna Land.

But if one listens closely, one can hear what is being said. To Flozell Adams, the offensive tackle Parcells had been cajoling to finally become all that he could be and then some, who collapses to the turf, clutching his right knee and writhing.

This was the same Adams who'd been one of the prime off-season projects for the Jock Whisperer. In 2002 Adams had been the cornerstone of a line that could have best served as the "be-fore" picture in one of those Slim Fast commercials in which Parcells had once appeared. The Michigan State product had become a too-gentle giant, a noncombatant. Yet he still managed to capture the spotlight of the TV cameras on frequent occasions throughout the season: "Holding. Number 76. Offense." Like Arnold Schwarzenegger, Flozell Adams had clearly mastered a gift for grab.

The Jock Whisperer had ascertained that Adams would not be responsive to the kind of stick-a-boot-up-their-ass motivational approach that works well with other players. Adams was one of those sensitive 350-pounders, the quiet type. Withdrawn. Had he been a Thoroughbred racehorse, the Jock Whisperer might have placed a goat in his stall for companionship, as trainer Tom Smith had attempted with Seabiscuit. But whatever the Jock Whisperer had whispered into Flozell Adams's

ear, the results were plain coming into this San Antonio training ordeal. Flozell had shed thirty-five pounds and arrived in
camp with an almost flat-bellied profile. He was in the best
shape of his life.

And now he's on the ground. Under previous administrations,
Adams would have limped off the field and been gone for a week.
Last season in San Antonio, it seemed that the players basking in
the training-room whirlpool outnumbered the players on the
practice field. Now things are different.

The fatherly Tuna stands over the big fella and softly offers a
sympathetic directive. "Get back in the fucking huddle," Parcells says.

Adams gets up and the workout continues. A long seven
months later, Flozell would make his first ever appearance in the
Pro Bowl.

At the conclusion of the morning drill, a media-player interchange takes place. Reporters are allowed to interview players at
the conclusion of the workout, in the area between the football
field and the tunnel that leads into the Alamodome locker room.
This makes for an odd scene, the sort of tribal mating ritual that
Margaret Mead found so fascinating in the deep jungles of Mi-
cronesia. Reporters, moving in like a school of piranha going after a dead hog that has fallen in the water, attach themselves to
the most media-worthy individuals on the roster, the Quincy
Carters and the Joey Galloways. Some are armed with notepads,
others with little handheld recorders, and some carry microphones on long poles. They form a ring around the player and
bombard him with questions. The players then supply the right
answers, which in Bill Parcells's football Kremlin are nonan-
swers. Quincy confirms that the team is trying to cut down on

mistakes. Now there's a scoop. Joey declares that he feels like he might have a pretty good season, unless he breaks his leg or something. Stop the presses!

Just for the hell of it, I join one of the circle dances—the man in the middle is Antonio Bryant, now entering his second season as a wide out. After five days, he was the only player to miss a workout. He was absent at the morning session when he flew back to Dallas to have surgery on a finger and was back in practice the same afternoon. According to Bryant's pre-Parcells reputation, the player who now wore Michael Irvin's number 88 was a twenty-three-year-old with the maturity of an eighth-grade window peeper. In the next-to-the-last game of the 2002 season against the Giants at the Meadowlands, the Cowboys had been humiliated. Trailing 0–31 in the game's final moments, the Giants allowed Dallas a mercy touchdown, a pass from Chad Hutchinson to Bryant. Antonio then established a new National Football League record for being the player to spike the ball over the goalpost crossbar when his team was most points behind. But his desire to become a star is unmistakable, and Bryant shows an almost uncontrollable eagerness to succeed that rises to the surface like bubbles in a hot kettle.

I decide to ask Bryant a question: "Antonio, now that you have a full NFL season under your belt, how is that going to help you improve this season?"

"Last year the pro game seemed real fast to me," he responds. "This year, the game seems, uh, like slower."

As far as quotes go, that was probably as provocative as anything a Cowboys player would tell the media. No, it was very clear that Big Bill himself was the sole spokesperson for this team. So I trotted back across the field and proceeded to the lower concourse of the Alamodome, where Parcells would address the media at his daily 11:30 press conference.

The Tuna might be the only guy doing the talking for this team, but he was saying plenty, giving command performances in what the reporters were now calling Bill's 11:30 Club.

It's 11:15, and the interview room is filling up. A bank of video cameras for the numerous TV outlets covering the camp is arranged along the back. I inspect one of the cameras and ask the guy who operates it how much the thing cost.

"Little over forty-five grand," he says. "This is a new model, the kind we used to cover the war in Iraq."

"You were in Iraq?"

"Oh, fuck no, man. You think I'm nuts?"

Now, five minutes before Bill's arrival, the room is packed. Parcells himself marvels at the sheer numbers. "There are more people here covering these workouts than came to my press conferences before playoff games when I was with the Giants," he says. These reporters all look serious. They are serious. These people in no way resemble the people who covered the Cowboys a generation ago, the guys who competed for the coveted Soup-Nose Award that went to the reporter who got the drunkest and made the biggest ass of himself the night before a road game.

The Soup-Nose Award was named in honor of a Dallas newspaper photographer back in the 1960s who joined a table occupied by Tom Landry and his wife, Alicia, at Bookbinder's Restaurant in Philadelphia. The man was gassed, and he never made it to his entrée, passing out, facedown, into his bowl of mock turtle soup. Alicia Landry detected some faint gurgling noises, and then Tom pulled his head from the bowl, saving the photographer from becoming the first drowning victim in a five-star restaurant. Thus the award.

But they probably quit giving out the Soup-Nose prize about twenty years ago, because there was nobody left in the press corps who had the raw talent to win it, the right stuff. The drunken poets of Texas's newspapers of yesteryear, the ones who would finish off a quart of Old Soak and then compose a lead paragraph that might read: "The time has come, the walrus said, to talk of many things. Of shoes and ships and sealing wax and the preposterous notion that Dallas will ever win a championship as long as Don Meredith is the quarterback," or, "Holy mackerel, Sapphire, look at the hair on that blocked punt!" Those guys are all dead now and gone with the mighty Texas wind. With Tom Landry no longer around to rescue them, a couple of them probably drowned.

Now, as the second hand on my railroad-approved Seiko watch hits the bull's-eye on 11:30, the Tuna makes his entry. Parcells—and this would be the first time I would see the man at close range—does indeed have what mystery author Raymond Chandler described as "the face and eyes of somebody you would probably want to get along with." Parcells was wearing shorts, and I noticed that he didn't have those golf-ball-sized knots in his calves that are supposed to be the trademark of NFL coaches. So Jerry Jones could have coached this team, after all. Oh well. Too late now.

It was time for the New Media to go to work. A member, a reporter from Fort Worth, grills Big Bill about how the practice reps would be divided among the running backs—Troy Hambrick, Aveion Cason, and Richie Anderson. Then and there, I wanted to scream out, "My God, Fort Worth boy. Don't you realize that nobody in your town, that nobody in the world, gives a shit about practice reps?"

Parcells gives an answer. Frankly, the Tuna is bewildered by all of the rabid attention that mainstream media are devoting to something as mundane as a football practice, where nothing really happens. The media-savvy Parcells, who is actually offering the appearance that he enjoys these 11:30 Club jamborees, is gracious enough to toss back something quotable from the practice rep question. He speaks of Cason, a snail darter of a halfback by NFL standards. "I'll tell ya what," Bill says. "The idea that Aveion Cason would be the featured running back in this offense or anybody else's—he'd finish the season in a coffin."

Somebody asks Parcells something about his secondary, and Bill, trying to stave off the boring, the inconsequential, takes the question and carries it into an area that, to the Tuna, is of far greater interest.

"There's a shortage of cornerbacks throughout football," he announces. "You know why? Because most of the players with the size and skills that it takes to be a great corner, they're all playing point guard somewhere. All along the big population centers on the East Coast, the inner-city high schools simply don't have the necessary funding to operate top-notch football programs. So the better athletes, they all play hoops, because they know that offers a better opportunity to play their sport at the next level, and perhaps the level beyond that."

One day later, the 11:30 Club media members have something new to gnaw upon.

The Cowboys' first preseason game at Arizona, and the reunion with Emmitt Smith looming at the end of the week, suddenly become secondary considerations. Once again, the quote from afar, and not the football game itself, becomes the top-of-the-marquee item.

Jeremy Shockey, red-hot media star with the New York Giants, has been popping off in print. Shockey actually has something in common with another Big Apple worship object from years gone by, Mickey Mantle. In civilian attire, they revert back to their true beings, that of ignorant-ass Oklahoma shit-kickers.

So Shockey has been the topic of a major feature in *New York* magazine. He talks about his desire to personally lead his Giants on a blitzkrieg through the league in the coming season, and one of the guys he particularly wants to beat is Bill Parcells, whom he then calls "the homo." That particular term—"homo," used in an obviously negative connotation—was one that I hadn't heard in that context since the playground in the fifth grade.

Back in San Antonio, the media demand a response. And what, exactly, is Parcells supposed to say? It takes one to know one, maybe? No, that won't work. In today's hyper–politically correct universe, any remark that the Tuna would make would have been the wrong one. So Bill (after thirty-nine years of marriage, he has probably been painted into a corner before) simply says, "I have no idea what you're talking about. I really don't."

Since I am allowed media access to Parcells and the Cowboys with a credential that says I am representing *Playboy,* I am keeping a low profile. Cowboys media relations people do not take kindly to people who are writing books, in which you can use words like "fuck."

This was the one point, however, where I was oh so tempted

to speak out and address the new coach of the Dallas Cowboys. I wanted to say, "Hey, Bill, if you *are* a homo, boy, did you come to the right town, because Big D not only has the world's greatest assembly of closet queens but also an endless supply of gerbil-stuffing, rump-wrangling, noodle-smooching, all-around K-Y cowboys. You'll really get a bang out of the Ned Beatty lookalike contest they have every Wednesday night down at the Rubber Glove Lounge on Cedar Springs."

Okay, I wanted to say that, but what the hell? This is supposed to be about pigskin, not porkskin.

CHAPTER 10

"SELL THIS F***ING TEAM NOW!"

If Parcells is out of step with any aspect of the modern generation of professional athlete, it lies in the fact that his body remains largely unpierced, and he does not wear any tattoos. If he did have a tattoo, if he wanted to be hip, the Tuna would have inscribed in purple ink one of his pet football phrases, Don't Tell Me About the Pain, Just Show Me the Baby, right over the barbed wire that encircles the right bicep.

Well, the baby that his new team, the Dallas Cowboys, hatched out in the Arizona desert in Parcells's debut in a competition that was supposed to present the trappings of game-day conditions, that baby was so ugly that the doctor slapped its momma. Quick, Nurse. Put a sack over its head. And would somebody get that squawking brat to shut up? Stick a sock in its mouth, and get it the fuck out of here.

Arizona offers unlimited capacity for calamity for anybody passing through. Unless your name happens to be Cochise or Geronimo, you've got no business out there in the first place. An eeriness lurks thick above the clouds of the region. That's fortified by a peculiar serenity that is not airbrushed but actually chiseled onto the faces of the natives, who appear to exist in a dream state that suggests, "Wake me when the killing starts." It always does, as evidenced by the gunfight at the OK Corral. Arizona is a place where you don't want to ask too many questions. Don Boles, a reporter for the *Arizona Republic,* learned that when some mob goons he was writing about put an explosive device in his car and blew his ass halfway to Bakersfield.

Those barren sands can be tougher on the body and soul than the jungles of the Amazon. In February 2004 a former regular traveler on the pro golf tour, Greg Kraft, actually filed a lawsuit against the PGA for allowing him to play in a couple of tournaments in the Grand Canyon State without warning him of the potential perils of desert fever. That's what they call a condition that might also be described as trench mouth of the lungs.

So it's not too unusual that the Cowboys would travel to Arizona and bomb. It's happened before. They'd lost their previous four regular-season games at Sun Devil Stadium in Tempe, and losing four straight to the Arizona Cardinals under any circumstances stands out as a breathtaking accomplishment. Yeah, back when Dallas was winning three Super Bowl games in four seasons, the Cowboys had beaten the Pittsburgh Steelers in Tempe to take the third one. Look what happened after that. It was as if the Cowboys picked up some kind of social disease during their Super Bowl week in Phoenix and carried the hex home with them, because team fortunes had been a downhill bobsled run ever since.

Arizona remains famous for its one lingering legend, which is rich in the horror stories that surround the destiny of people who went in search of the Lost Dutchman Mine. Yet the haunted souls that used to occupy the bleached skeletal remains of those tragic fortune hunters would whisper from the great beyond that if they had to do it all over, they'd go look for the mine again before they'd take the job as head coach of those goofy-ass football Cardinals.

If coaching the Cincinnati Bengals serves as a dead-end street careerwise, then running the Arizona program is a one-way highway that leads straight off a cliff. Pro football and the Valley of the Sun simply don't mix. Fortunately for the franchise, the stadium is not that far from Mesa, which serves as the southern-most power base for the disciples of the Church of the Latter-Day Saints. So those Mormons bring all of their wives to watch the Cardinals in all of their futility; otherwise that team would be lucky to draw two thousand fans a game.

Despite the dismal karma that had encircled the Cowboys in previous visits, Parcells and his players had traveled west with some ambitions of making a decent showing. That was based on what Parcells had seen after two weeks' worth of the two-a-day workout grind at the Alamodome in San Antonio. Parcells, while quick to emphasize that he had no real idea of what this team might have to offer, had indeed thrown some indications that he might have located a pulse during the practices. He had hinted as much during his boot camp. The only real setback to date had been a knee injury to the rookie center Al Johnson, whose mean streak had been impressing the Tuna and his staff. Johnson's knee would sideline him for the season and perhaps beyond.

But a defensive tackle, Willie Blade, was helping offset the disappointment over the loss of Johnson, and this was at a spot where Parcells needed help more desperately than at center. Willie Blade served as a living example of Parcells, the Jock Whisperer, at his very best. Blade's most memorable moment in Dallas, after being selected in the third round of the 2001 draft from Mississippi State, had happened when he'd shit in his pants during a practice session. His pro career had hardly been uphill from there on. Blade had missed a season with a dislocated wrist, been released by the Cowboys, and signed on with the Houston Texans for 2002 but was never activated, not even for one game by a horseshit expansion team, and, in the spring of 2003, found himself back in Dallas.

Prior to a conditioning drill, Parcells asked Blade how much he weighed. "Three-twenty, Coach," Blade said.

"Really?" answered Parcells. "Let's see." In front of the entire squad, Parcells marched Blade to the scales. Then, taking on an expression of mock wonderment, he declared, "Gosh, son. That's amazing. In that short little walk across this room, you just gained thirty pounds!" Later, Parcells would phone Willie Blade's father back in Warner Robbins, Georgia, and ask the man to implore his son to lose weight, because the kid's pro future was at stake, and third chances happen very rarely in life and never in the National Football League.

The Jock Whisperer, once again, had done it. In a controlled scrimmage against the Houston Texans in San Antonio, one week prior to the Arizona trip, Blade was in the starting lineup.

On the first play, he not only made a tackle for a four-yard loss, he also made good on that rare third chance.

Parcells had singled out Antonio Bryant, the receiver cloaked with the problem-child reputation, as typical of what he had seen in these practices that served as the prelude for the Big Circus that would start in what, before the kickoff at Tempe, was just less than a month away. "When he went and had his hand operated on and was back on the field at two-thirty the same afternoon for the second workout of the day, that showed me something, and I told the team that," Parcells said. "Yeah, it wasn't open-heart surgery. Just his pinkie, but that's the attitude that I like. This guy is a gifted athlete, and he's ambitious. Bryant has this knock on him, that he's supposed to be a headstrong kinda guy. I've had headstrong players, and there's nothing wrong with that, as long as it's properly contained.

"And I've seen that out of a bunch of these guys. Just yesterday, I was watching the whole squad out there on the field, stretching before practice, the whole damn team, and I did not see a single player at any point during two-a-days, where I'd thought to myself, 'You know, I wish that SOB wasn't here.'

"Another thing I like is that we have some guys competing for positions who can help us on special teams, too. That's important to me. I love working with special teams. It's my favorite part of the game, really. Remember what Colonel Red Blaik used to say? No? You don't remember Colonel Blaik? Well, he used to coach at West Point, coached two Heisman Trophy winners, Glenn Davis and Doc Blanchard . . . Mr. Inside and Mr. Outside, they called 'em . . . and later he had Vince Lombardi on his staff, and what Colonel Blaik used to say was, 'Let's put the "foot" back into "football."'

"I've seen some teams in this league who kept guys around because of their potential as position players, but couldn't play on the special teams, and it's hurt 'em. And they didn't know it was hurtin', apparently, because they kept on doing it." Pure Parcells-ese. So if the Tuna was not exactly bursting with optimistic energy for the game with Arizona, it seemed that he had detected at least some flickers of hope. "I wake up in the middle of the night, thinking about this or that, worrying about various details, and I can't go back to sleep," he said of his San Antonio experience. "And while I am mad that I can't go back to sleep, it makes me happy that at this point in my life, I can still get excited, get worked up about the job."

This would be the last time Parcells would comment on his middle-of-the-night agonies until the season was over, and after the Arizona exhibition, it was easy to see why. The offensive lineup that would start the game in Tempe would essentially be the same one that would open the regular season against Atlanta and remain in place for the whole year.

Wide receivers, Antonio Bryant and Terry Glenn. (Joey Galloway would sit this one out.)

Interior line: Flozell Adams, Larry Allen, Matt Lehr, Andre Gurode, and Ryan Young.

Tight end: Dan Campbell.

Running back: Troy Hambrick.

Fullback: Richie Anderson.

Quarterback: Chad Hutchinson, the one glaring example of a player who would not appear very much more and, in fact, appeared exactly one quarter of one game during the regular season.

Now, with game conditions fully in place, with league-certified zebras at work and time-outs mandated by TV, Bill Parcells could finally see the two quarterbacks, Hutchinson and Carter, at work under conditions in which the coach could apply his own analysis and prognosis. He'd implored reporters to assure their avid listeners and readers to place no value whatsoever in Hutchinson's getting the first-quarter assignment in this largely meaningless preseason fling. The media weren't listening, since, with the exception of the crazed heretic at Dallas's Channel 8, Dale Hansen, they'd all placed the starter's tiara on Hutchinson's lily-white head. They would brook no argument to the contrary, even from Parcells himself.

So Hutchinson trotted on the field to begin the game, and his first offensive series went like this.

- First down: Hutchinson pass to Bryant, incomplete.
- Second down: Anderson up the middle for five yards.
- Third down: Hutchinson pass incomplete to Glenn.
- Fourth down: Toby Gowin, thirty-nine-yard punt.

Arizona's quarterback, the veteran Jeff Blake, was making his first start in the desert. Jake "the Snake" Plummer, the fixture at Tempe in previous seasons, was in Denver now. Once Plummer had become eligible for a free-agent ticket, he'd skipped town like an inmate fleeing Alcatraz on the rubber raft somebody had given him for his birthday. Blake completed a few passes in his first turn. One of them was an eleven-yarder to Emmitt Smith, who appeared only long enough to show the Cardinal fans how stylish he looked in his new red jersey and sat out the rest of the game. Blake drove the Cardinals deep enough into the Dallas territory for a Bill Gramatica field goal and a 3–0 lead.

Back came Hutchinson.

- First down: Hambrick over left tackle for a minus two yards.
- Second down: Hutchinson pass complete to Anderson for a minus four yards.
- Third down: Hutchinson pass incomplete to Bryant.
- Fourth down: Toby Gowin, forty-six-yard punt.

Oh, well. Look at the bright side. Hutchinson appeared to have solved his chronic fumbling problem, although he still hadn't been hit.

On Dallas's next possession, with the Cowboys pinned back at their own three, matters, momentarily, would appear less grim.

- First down: Hutchinson pass to Bryant, eight yards.
- Second down: Hambrick around left end for minus two.
- Third down: Aveion Cason over right guard for twelve yards.
- First down: Hutchinson pass to Glenn for fifteen yards.
- First down: Hambrick, left tackle, one yard.
- Second down: Hutchinson hit four yards behind the line of scrimmage by Ray Thompson. Fumble. Fumble recovered by Arizona's Kenny King.

Oh, shit. When Hutchinson trotted off the field, Parcells offered him a noncommittal shrug. During the entire tenure of Tuna's coaching career, he had only once become so angry with a player that he had "actually felt like doing something about it." That had happened during his more tempestuous years, back when Parcells was moving from town to town like a migrant prune-picker.

Yet, there seemed to be a flicker around the corners of Parcells's mouth as Hutchinson sat down that suggested he might be stifling some hidden desire to place both thumbs against Chad's windpipe and press down as hard as he could. That's a technique that criminal pathologists clinically refer to as manual strangulation. It was best that Big Bill hadn't acted on his emotions, because as the game continued, he may have had to croak Quincy Carter as well, and then what? Call Phil Simms.

The vital numbers that would be posted at the end of the wasted night out in the warm desert breeze were too deplorable for Parcells to bother to even examine. The third-stringer, Tony Romo, had the best stats. The Cardinals won, by the way, 13–0.

After the game, Parcells sought out Jerry Jones in the Dallas locker room and initiated a conversation.

"Hey, Jerry," Parcells said. "Who handles your financial affairs for you? You know. Gives you investment advice?"

"Well, shit, Bill, I handle that myself," Jones said. "You know that. Everybody knows it."

"Okay. Then let me give you a little insider-trading tip," Parcells went on.

"Oh, yeah? What's that?"

"Sell the team! Sell this fuckin' team now! Sell it while there's still some value! Sell it while the sellin's good!"

Later Parcells would describe his entire team's performance as "a dog's lunch. It was a mess." Of course, most of us would rather order the dog's lunch than the Tuna casserole that was served up cold in Tempe.

★　　★　　★

The following week, Bill Parcells made his world premiere—preseason style—on the Cowboys sideline against the Houston Texans. The kickoff temperature was at ninety-five degrees with high humidity, and many players on both teams—during the half and after the game—would be hydrated via IVs. And this was one of those typical August Texas nights on which the players would actually squeeze the bag to accelerate the flow of the fluid. Dallas won, 34–6. But that was only because the Texans played like the team that they actually were, a warmed-over expansion franchise that played a lot of close games simply because of the mediocrity—otherwise known as parity—that had descended across the league via free agency and expansion.

After a trip to Pittsburgh, where Dallas lost, 15–14, Parcells, with the regular-season opener looming ever closer, examined his personnel and was perplexed by all aspects but two in particular.

The first was Larry Allen, his left guard. Here was a player who not only would be described by John Madden as the best in history at his position but who also had been voted onto the NFL all-decade team of the 1990s. And he was regarded as the strongest man ever to play professional football. (He could bench-press over seven hundred pounds and had a squat lift of nine hundred pounds.) Now he wasn't practicing, complaining of nonspecific injuries, and Parcells couldn't figure out why. In San Antonio, Allen had spent so much time off the field riding the exercise bike that the Tuna finally presented him with a yellow jersey, the kind that Lance Armstrong wears.

Allen's decline as a player had become a source of concern during the 2002 campaign, when he had taken an instant dislike to the zone-blocking routine that had been established by offensive coordinator Bruce Coslet in his failed attempt to install a West Coast offense in Dallas. When Tom Landry was coaching the Cowboys, he'd approached defensive tackle Jethro Pugh at halftime of some long-ago game and said, "Jethro, that guy you're playing against is outthinking you." Pugh replied, "That's all right. By the end of the game, he'll be as stupid as I am."

That embodied the approach to the sport that Larry Allen had embraced while constructing his career as "the most decorated offensive lineman in Cowboys history." From the first play of every game on, his intent was simply to eventually force the player on the opposite side of the line to quit. The passive technique involved with the zone-blocking plan was taking the fun out of the sport for Larry Allen. According to what I will call "a source close to the team," "Allen approached [line coach] Tom Verducci and said, 'This zone thing won't work. All I want to do is to fuck my guy up, and this way, I can't do it.' Allen wasn't buying into the scheme, plus he was hurt. Allen was getting old, he had a laundry list of personal problems that ran from here to Fresno, and he was reaching the point where his body was starting to tell him, like with us all, that it really didn't give a shit anymore. And you know who else didn't give a shit about Allen's personal problems and all of his aches and pains? Bill Parcells."

Out of deference to who Larry Allen was and still might be, the Tuna was forcing himself to remain patient. Maybe it was time to retire the old Clydesdale and send him out to stud. But the Jock Whisperer inside Parcells told him that there was still something left of Larry Allen the football player and that he could and would go jaw to jaw with a few more defensive tackles and fuck 'em up but good, just for old times' sake.

The other concern, and the one more pressing, was the quarterback issue. Neither Hutchinson nor Carter had been moving ahead, or behind really, in the competition to determine which player would start. Carter, Parcells knew, was not as bad as previously advertised. In truth, the public and media perception of Quincy Carter had been tainted by the mere fact that Jerry Jones had handpicked him from the draft.

This was the same Jerry Jones who had presided over a sequence of top picks who were to become serial flops, aka Jerry's Kids. Shante Carver. Kavika Pittman. David LeFleur. Ebenezer Ekuban. And, of course, the Joey Galloway-for-two-first-rounders swap. Had Quincy Carter been the product of a Jimmy Johnson regime—back when the Cowboys were pulling the long-odds guys from Nowheresville out of their ass, people such as Erik Williams and Leon Lett, not to mention Larry Allen—Quincy Carter would have been perceived differently. "Just watch. In his third season, this cat will win ten games." That's what Mel Kuiper, Jr., and the rest of the self-ordained draft analysts would have said.

Hutchinson? Hell, if he didn't fumble every third play, he seemed on the verge of displaying potential. If Parcells was telling the media he still had no clue as to the player with the inside track, he was being honest. "I'm just looking for a guy who can drive the bus," he said. And the following day, when pressed on the matter, he would elaborate. "Contrary to what most people think, there is a lot more to playing quarterback than dropping back and throwing the ball. There's continuity and flow and timing, all this stuff. In baseball, you know, nothing happens until the pitcher pitches the ball. And if the batter swings, after that, everybody reacts. Football isn't that way. Football isn't like that. In football, everybody has to start at the same time. It's like a symphony. If the tuba starts before the violin, it doesn't sound too good."

Poor Bill. First he needs a bus driver, then he wants a symphony conductor. The quarterback he is looking for is half Ralph Kramden, half Leonard Bernstein.

Finally, in the workout after a practice that followed the Houston game, Hutchinson would solve Parcells's quarterback question. Hutchinson approached the Tuna and asked, "What's my role going to be?"

Meeting with the media later in the week, Parcells, complaining about a variety of features on the team that had been giving him stomach cramps, said, "And now I have players coming up to me and [mimicking in a whiny voice] asking 'What's my role?' And to them I say, 'Why in the hell don't you show me something? Then, maybe you can have a role.'" A day later, Parcells would issue what amounted to a local bombshell. "Quincy will start the Oakland game [the final preseason match, set at Texas Stadium]. He might play the whole game this time. If he goes out, maybe Tony Romo will come in. Hutchinson isn't going to play against Oakland."

Dallas overwhelmed Oakland, 52–13, and while this was still preseason, it was an outcome that guaranteed one determination. Nobody knew how good Dallas might be, but the Raiders were damn sure not going back to the Super Bowl for a second straight season.

The next game on the schedule was against Atlanta, and this was the first one that would count. The fact that Michael Vick was out with a broken leg offered no comfort to Parcells. After months of preparation, the Tuna, with his corps of midget linebackers and a mystery man at quarterback, was about to enter the mists, and he felt that he was surrounded by strangers. So what the hell. He's the one who'd seen Jerry Jones on the TV monitor just over eight months earlier and said, "I could work for a guy like that." It was too late to turn back now.

CHAPTER 11

THE DAWN OF THE AGE OF THE TUNA

With the Dallas–Fort Worth metropolitan area soon to be ordained as the nation's third fattest population center, it was symbolic that on this Sunday afternoon in early September 2003 it became a celebration of clogged arteries.

In this case, I refer to the traffic that jammed the major thoroughfares that drained into Texas Stadium. The dawning of the Bill Parcells Era was at hand. Parcells's tenure with the Dallas Cowboys might be destined to extend for a triumphant decade, or it might unravel after a half season. Who knew? Since this was the almighty Tuna, however, no matter the outcome, his coming would be remembered as an era.

It was Sunday, and like the people driving to church a few

hours earlier, the fans inching toward Jerry Jones's Football Gospel Temple were divided into two theological camps—the skeptics and the true believers. Everyone in this congregation was united on one front, however. The new man in the pulpit, Parcells, had some serious preaching to do.

Texas Stadium has provided the stage for some seriously memorable and dramatic passion plays in its past. Five NFC championship games were performed in this arena, with its curious hole in the roof that allowed, according to local legend, a better view for God to watch God's team.

The stadium resounds with enriching memories. Here was where Clint Longley, the so-called Mad Bomber, had come off the bench to rally the Cowboys to an unlikely win over the Redskins in 1974. Here was where defensive end Harvey Martin heaved a funeral wreath into the Redskins' dressing room after the Cowboys had knocked them out of the playoffs with an astounding comeback in the final regular-season game of 1979. One week after that, in a playoff game against the Los Angeles Rams, Roger Staubach was taking his customary walk across the water—and sank. The last pass of Roger's fabled career was thrown in that game. It hit Dallas offensive guard Herb Scott in the butt, and Staubach then retired. In the Rams' dressing room after that game, I heard Jack "Hacksaw" Reynolds refer to the Cowboys' flamboyant Hollywood Henderson as "Texas Butch." It was in the summer of 1984 that the stadium was jammed with its largest crowd ever, for—guess what?—a Michael Jackson concert. The parking lot was overflowing with tricycles. Who could ever forget the Thanksgiving game against Miami in 1993—Ice Bowl II—when Leon Lett stupidly skidded across the frozen artificial ground cover and into a spinning live ball after a blocked field goal, a blunder that would give the Dolphins the freakiest of possible victories?

Bill Parcells's Dallas Cowboys regular-season opener against Atlanta would mark the beginning of the thirty-second season of football at Texas Stadium. But like the bare-midriffed cheerleaders who dance within, the place was seriously over the hill at age twenty-one. It had started to look a little, well, saggy, with a few stretch marks here and there, with wrinkles appearing around its eyes and mouth and gray streaks up around the top. It was beginning to need too much makeup. This edifice that looked like such a sparkling sugarcoated Easter egg when it opened now more resembled one of those organic brown eggs you see in the natural-food grocery store. The deteriorating quality of the North Texas air, over the passage of the years, has coated the once-proud coliseum with what might pass for tobacco stains. So rather than bringing in a cosmetic dentist for a whitening procedure, Jerry Jones was actively politicking for a new venue entirely. This joint was too far gone for a face-lift, right, Jerry? Since his preoccupation would limit his time to devote to the football end of the Cowboys' operation, it might be speculated that the declining nature of Texas Stadium, and Jones's devotion to the cause of building a new palace, were the catalysts that brought Parcells to the Cowboys. Jerry would be awfully busy in negotiations with Laura Miller, the mayor of Dallas, in efforts to create a stadium tax district that would fund the new Jonestown. Since Laura Miller is the sort of mayor who screams at homeless people, insisting that they get off the streets of her city and get the hell out of her sight, Jones knew that the task of bonding with this particular politician would prove, uh, demanding.

That might take months, even years. So the notion was, in

Jerry's thought process, "Let's just let the Tuna run this football show until I get back."

How could he go wrong?

I was at Texas Stadium for its official grand opening in 1971, the season the Cowboys won their first Super Bowl. Duane Thomas scored the first touchdown in the history of the stadium, against the New England Patriots. It was about a sixty-five-yarder. Thomas would refer to Tom Landry as "Plastic Man" that season, but Landry didn't care. Thomas could have called him Jane Fonda, as long as he ran with the ball the way he did.

My job that day had been to interview Jim Plunkett—fresh out of Stanford with his Heisman trophy and all—and talk about the perils that befell the rookie quarterback in the NFL. I don't remember anything about my conversation with Plunkett. What I do remember is the press-box amenities of the new stadium. Every writer had his (there were no hers in the sports media of that era) own swivel chair, with genuine tan leather. What a contrast to the previous setup at the Cotton Bowl, where all the writers sat crammed, asshole to elbow, on little wooden bar stools.

At this new Texas Stadium, the print journalists were completely segregated from the broadcast people—the talking dogs. They had their own press box, way over on the other side of the field, the east side. We, the ink-stained wretches, applauded the setup. The writers regarded the broadcasters as an inferior caste. In our thinking they were lepers, the fools, and we somehow suspicioned that they made four times our salaries. Another media feature that Tex Schramm, that all-knowing impresario of the show business that pro football had truly become, had introduced at this new Texas Stadium facility was press-box "attendants." These were fresh-faced young girls attired along the lines of the cheerleaders. Their uniforms were somewhat more sedate, but the hot pants and white boots and cute little teardrop asses were part of the ensemble. Their job was to bring the sportswriters cold beer or—what the hell?—a scotch and soda, if they wanted one.

Naturally, I cannot count the times I have returned to this place over the thirty-two years since Tex first unlocked and opened wide those swinging doors to his gentlemen's club for sportswriters. Now, in 2003, as I approached the stadium for the Tuna's debut against Dan Reeves's Falcons in what might have been the first NFL game ever to match two head coaches who'd survived heart bypass operations, I was finally to experience something new, something strange.

The doddering fool, that being me, had neglected to obtain the parking pass that accompanied the press-box credential. That meant that leaving for the stadium about an hour sooner than usual would be the prudent course. But what the hell? Here was an opportunity for a new experience, a chance to go and rub bellies with the real people, the true fans. Yet, as I followed the arrows on the signs that read "Public Parking $12," a feeling of queasiness, a sensation of hidden danger, a tightening of the throat, among other areas, were beginning to take hold. "Public Parking." The subliminal message was clear. "Head Lice Parking Just Ahead." "Quarantine Lot for SARS Patients Only." Those arrows were not pointing toward Texas Stadium but directing me off in another direction. Uh-oh. Instead of the Blue Lot, where the nice people who own season tickets park, the proletariat of the public parking steerage—the peons, the outcasts—were being herded in the opposite direction, back behind the Central Freight Yard, where acres of battle-weary big rigs were situated.

I paid the $12, felt relieved that a letter from a probation officer was not a requirement for admission, drove over a bridge, and then, there it was . . . a vast, unpaved field, stretching all the way to the eastern horizon, crammed and chock-full of cars packed together like bees in a hive, while a cloud of smoke hovered just above. The smoke was from the campfires, where the public parkers had been cooking squirrels and possums impaled on sticks.

> We look out at the barbarian host, who in the slanting gray light mass like figures in a nightmare. Their hair (both head and face) is uncut, vilely dressed with oil, braided into abhorrent shapes. Their bodies are distorted by ornament and discolored by paint. Some of the men are huge and muscular to the point of deformity, their legs wrapped comically in the garments called braccae—breeches. There is no discipline among them; they bellow at each other and race about in chaos. They are dirty, and they stink. A crone in a filthy blanket stirs a cauldron, slicing roots and rancid meat into the concoction from time to time. She slices a carrot crosswise up its shaft, so that the circular pieces she cuts off float like foolish yellow eyes on the surface of the brew.

Actually, that was Thomas Cahill, describing the Germanic hordes that would overrun the Roman Empire in *How the Irish Saved Civilization*. Well, Cahill might have thought he was writing about the people who would deliver Western civilization into the Dark Ages, but what Cahill was truly describing was public parking, Texas Stadium, circa 2003.

Gripped with apprehension, I drove my Jeep Cherokee slowly, reluctantly, almost tenderly into this savage encampment. At once, I was assaulted by a group of six or more tailgaters from the depths of hell. They pounded the Jeep with their fists. I anticipated that I would be dragged from the Jeep and have my skull bashed in with a brick.

"Hey, cocksucker! Are you a Cowboys fan!?"

I tried to remember what the park ranger at Yellowstone had recommended if I ever hiked upon a mother grizzly bear protecting her cubs. Oh, that's right. She said that the one thing to do, one's only chance to avoid being mauled to death and eaten, was to shout, "You're goddamn right I'm a Cowboys fan! Fuck the Falcons!"

Well, it worked. I was allowed to pass and, without additional further attack, finally located a narrow slot to park the Jeep, out near the most distant perimeter of the public lot. I was probably closer to my house in Dallas than to Texas Stadium. By now, only forty-five minutes remained until the kickoff, and I would have to practically jog the three or so miles that separated me from the press gate in order to make it.

When it comes to mingling among the rustics at a crowd scene, I thought that I had been to the mountaintop when I toured the encampment of fans situated on the wooded hillside that adjoins the Martinsville Motor Speedway, the evening before the Goody's Headache Powder 500. These Cowboys fans were even more impaired than the NASCAR junkies. Those race fans, though, they're a sadly divided bunch—the Earnhardts versus the Gordons, the Fords against the Chevys. Et cetera. But there's a spirit of common union that binds the Cowboys fans. One for all, and all for the Tuna. This felt like family.

It was suddenly an emancipating sensation, a cleansing of a sort, to be here among this immense herd of humanity gathered out here like worshippers at the banks of the Ganges on a holy day. These folks were wasted, many suffering from the blind staggers, and not a few others seemingly afflicted with the condition known as jake leg. That's a neurological condition that became rampant in Southern states during the dismal Prohibition days of the 1930s, caused by the consumption of contaminated bottles of Jamaican extract of ginger, or jake, where the victims were forced to walk in a high-stepping, foot-slapping style.

But there is a certain ingenuousness, an aura of sweetness about the jake leg set, that is all too lacking in the swells who were up there occupying the Texas Stadium luxury suites, sipping their piña coladas. That was an inspirational exhibition, this army of jake leggers, each and every soldier clad in officially licensed National Football League garb, stumbling en masse toward the stadium. It was a scene right out of *Dr. Zhivago*.

Sadly and all too soon, I would abandon their proud company and retreat back into the chilling isolation of the Texas Stadium press box. Those same tan leather swivel chairs that were so impressive to the kid sportswriter back in 1971, they were still there. So, in fact, were some of the same people who had been sitting in them. Had they changed much? Only to the extent that Jimmy Olson had, through the passage of years, turned into Andy Rooney. The writers were mostly assembled in a lounge area, watching the final minutes of the Giants-Rams game, gazing blankly at the screen. There was no interchange among them, much less the banter that used to characterize the press-box atmosphere of old, back when the sportswriters enjoyed their jobs. The columnists and the beat guys, they all appeared dazed, somehow institutionalized, as if they'd just been released from a twenty-year sentence at Betty Ford.

What was conspicuously missing from those early days were the beverage girls, not to mention the beverages themselves. There was a time in my career when that would have mattered. Now, the priorities had shifted substantially. I was here for the sole purpose of watching the Fourth Coming of Bill Parcells, and the soprano trill of an actual, on-duty Dallas Cowboys cheerleader singing "The Star-Spangled Banner" was the signal that the Tuna's time in Texas was soon at hand.

I was armed with facts:

- In three previous debut performances, Parcells was 1–2. He'd lost his first ever game as the Giants' head coach in 1983 to the L.A. Rams, 11–6. Ten years later, when he took over the Patriots, the Tuna had gotten whopped again, 38–10, but he'd won his premier effort with the Jets in 1997, beating Seattle 41–3.

- The team that Parcells was suiting up to face in Atlanta included thirty-three holdovers from the group that had lost so ignominiously at Houston the year before. The newcomers included five free-agent signees, five rookie free agents, four 2003 draft choices, three who had been added via trade, and three free-agent signees.

- Terence Newman would become the third rookie ever to start at cornerback in a season opener for Dallas, joining Ron Francis in 1987 and Kareem Larrimore in 2000. (This did not seem to bode particularly well for Terence Newman.)

- Flozell Adams would be starting his sixty-fifth consecutive game for the Cowboys, the longest active streak on the club.

- The Cowboys, counting this game, would have played in

front of 206 sold-out stadiums in their last 211 games, including 104 consecutive games at Texas Stadium.

None of which meant bat excrement to Bill Parcells. I focused my trusty Bushnell binoculars on the Tuna's face as Toby
Gowin prepared to kick off the season, and attempted to read his
thoughts. Given his grave countenance—the look of a man
standing at the altar and about to say "I do" to a proposition that
he'd wished he'd reconsidered before it was too late—one might
have guessed that the Tuna was thinking about something he'd
discussed at one of his soul-baring press conferences back in
San Antonio.

That was when Parcells related something that Al Davis had
told him about the unhappy reality of head coaching in the NFL:
"You know, there are going to be times when you are driving this
train and you're in a dark tunnel. And sitting behind you are your
players and your coaches, and also your general manager and the
owners of your franchise. They're all sitting there watching you
and they're all screaming and yelling at you, wanting to know
what in the hell is going on.

"And there are going to be times when you just can't turn
around and explain to 'em. You've got to just drive till you get out
of the tunnel—or till you wreck the train, one way or another."

How bitterly ironic that (ordinarily I would say unbeknownst
to the Tuna, except that I learned that there is choice little that is
unbeknownst to this man) the largest crowd to watch a sporting
event in the history of Texas paid to watch a train wreck. That
happened in the 1890s when a master showman staged the head-
on collision of two unmanned steam locomotives in a field near
Waco. The event was a huge box-office success, although artisti-

cally, the reviews were mixed. The boilers of both engines exploded on impact, and several spectators were scalded to death or killed by flying shrapnel.

Atlanta took the opening kickoff and drove for a field goal.

On the second offensive possession of the Tuna Regime, the Cowboys responded. Behind two crunching blocks thrown by the Jock Whisperer's two prime off-season projects—big Flo and Larry Allen—halfback Aveion Cason, the player that Parcells guaranteed would wind up in a coffin if he got too many carries, ripped through the hole, cut back to his right, and sprinted sixty-three yards for a touchdown.

For the remainder of the half, it seemed that the Cowboys, at any moment, were poised to land the knockout punch on these Falcons, a Vick-less bunch if I'd ever seen one. Then, the little annoyances that cause the Tuna's coronary arteries to constrict began to occur. A forty-eight-yard Quincy Carter to Joey Galloway completion that would have put the ball inside the Falcons' ten-yard line was wiped out by a motion penalty.

Toward the end of the half, the Cowboys had driven close to the Falcons' goal line, seemingly poised to carry a 14–3 lead into halftime. Tight end Dan Campbell, he of the hometown with the dinosaur tracks, ran a second down crossing pattern in the Atlanta end zone. He was momentarily open, about as open as a receiver is supposed to get in an NFL end zone, but Carter threw the ball behind his receiver, and Campbell, twisting around, was unable to make the catch.

Dallas would have to settle for a chip-shot field goal that would at least be worth a 10–3 intermission advantage—except that Billy Cundiff missed the kick, and suddenly Bill Parcells's tunnel was now a very dark place indeed. More frustrating yet was that in the second quarter Larry Allen, the Clydesdale, was off the field and on the bench, although there were no sideline reports of injury. What was wrong with Allen? Apparently, big number 73 was the only person in the stadium who could answer that, and he wasn't telling as he sat there like a 350-pound chocolate sundae, slowing melting in the early-September Texas sunshine. And at $8.8 million a season, this was the absolutely top-priced interior-line chocolate sundae in the entire league.

The second half, largely, was a fiasco. Atlanta cruised down the field for two touchdowns in the third quarter and kicked a field goal. Against the Falcons' running attack in the final thirty minutes of the game, the Incredible Hulks of the defense that Parcells so covets had performed like the Invisible Men. That legion of football "investors" who opted for the "under" in the Las Vegas proposition of a six-and-a-half-win season was already icing down the Dom Pérignon. Finally, in the fourth quarter, the Cowboys stirred back to life. Carter connected with Galloway for a long TD. Then Cundiff missed the PAT! Holy shit! In the late 1990s, the Cowboys' place kicker was named Richie "Happy Days" Cunningham. Now they were stuck with Beaver Cleaver. Send this little turkey back to Drake, and get Tom Dempsey on the phone!

The Beav's, uh, Cundiff's misfire didn't really matter. The Cowboys' defense, undersized and obviously gassed in the Texas September heat, was helpless as the Falcons drove the ball, drained the clock, and finally scored. Final: Dallas 13, Silly Vickless Team from Atlanta 27.

With minutes to play, the press-box folk evacuated to the elevator that would transport them to the dressing room area. The Tuna was situated in a side room, sitting at a table. His postgame demeanor was that of a person completely unamazed by what he had just witnessed. He realized all too well the inevitability of the consequences of the misfires his team had committed, all at the least opportune of times, against the Falcons.

Somebody asked Parcells about Larry Allen's departure from the field near the end of the first half. Was he hurt? Parcells could only shrug. "You can't put yourself inside another person's body," he responded.

So what concerned the Tuna the most about the team, in his Texas coaching debut? "We had the lead at the half, playing at home, and then we didn't even *act like* we wanted to do anything after that. Atlanta ran the ball almost at will in the second half. I told the team after the game that if we don't improve there, we won't win many games. If any."

Then, Parcells would note, rather prophetically, "We've got fifteen other games yet to play, just like this one, and this team won't be judged by this game today. It'll be judged by what happens over the course of the whole season."

Cason, the halfback, analyzed his team's showing in the argot of the modern professional athlete. "We had our opportunities," Cason said. "But we kept stabbing ourselves in the foot."

I felt as if I'd been stabbed in both feet as I trudged back to the public parking lot. That field behind the Central Freight Yard was vacant now but for a few abandoned wayfarers who had missed their ride and been left there for dead. The setting sun was to my back, and its reflection on the vast ocean of glass containers in that field offered the same glittering sparkle that you would get in the parking lot next door to the Dallas jail.

CHAPTER 12

ON THE SHOULDERS
OF GIANTS

New York City, according to popular urban legend, is a place where one works like a Japanese in order to live like a Russian. What then of the wretched labor caste in, say, Sandusky, Ohio, and Mansfield, Louisiana, and Clovis, New Mexico, and the remainder of the communities that dot the American landscape, most of whom, it might come as a shock to the overstressed New Yorker to learn, work every bit as hard as they do and cannot even find end-of-the-day comfort in Simon and Garfunkel's immortal whores of Forty-second Street?

Sometime around midyear 1969, in an office tower that overlooked the Avenue of the Americas, Roone Arledge was considering their plight and devising a plan to ease the burden of the "tote that bale" set and to cut the workweek by 20 percent. The concept of *Monday Night Football,* if that could be accomplished, might serve to wash some of the blue out of Mondays during those long three months that precede the end of another year.

Arledge was emerging as a programming exec with depth and gaining clout at the American Broadcasting Company that year. The problem that Arledge and his colleagues faced during those simpler precable years, when only three networks had the national TV landscape from sea to shining sea all to themselves, was that ABC struggled as the third-string network. It was a distant third, at that.

CBS was *I Love Lucy, Gunsmoke, What's My Line,* and Walter Cronkite. NBC was *Bonanza* and Bob Hope and Chet Huntley and David Brinkley. ABC was *Land of the Giants* and a steady stream of all but invisible sitcoms and failed drama series that were memorable only to the extent of how quickly they were forgotten.

Pete Rozelle, the NFL commissioner, had originally hatched the notion of telecasting an extra game on Monday night. To that point, every Sunday in the fall the National Football League had provided the video Thorazine that prevented Americans from hacking one another to pieces with machetes as the weeks of autumn arrived and the sadistically cold and barren winter lay ahead. It was only right that football should have a home on Monday nights as well. So he approached CBS, which nixed the idea. Its Monday night lineup was solid already. Next, Rozelle would inquire at NBC, which expressed marginal interest until Johnny Carson went through the ceiling. A game that ran long might preempt time from his *Tonight Show,* so fuck the NFL. Then Rozelle contacted his third and last resort. ABC needed something novel to attract viewer interest, something that by industry standards would be regarded as revolutionary.

That would require a project that was original, a product that combined entertainment value and immediacy, with slices of irreverence and controversy along the way. Arledge, whose background was on the news side of the network as opposed to the entertainment programmers who owned a 100 percent monopoly of the prime-time viewing hours of that era, had seen something intriguing in the summer of 1968.

Amid the turbulence of the Democratic National Convention in Chicago, all three networks offered wall-to-wall coverage, from Monday morning until Friday night of both parties' conventions in those days. It was the news department's only chance to slip onstage during the preciously prime evening viewing hours. That happened only every four years.

Again, CBS had Cronkite and its armada of other great correspondents like Roger Mudd and Mike Wallace, and NBC, again, came not only with Huntley and Brinkley, but John Chancellor, Sandor Vanocur, and the like. ABC? Peter Jennings was still probably in junior high school in 1968 and would serve as little use to the network. So needing something novel that might capture viewer attention, a diversion from the standard coverage—reporter breathlessly chasing swing-state Governor So-and-so across the convention hall floor—the people at ABC hatched a plan.

Each night, the ABC cameras, as a prelude to all of the speechmaking, would telecast face-to-face debates that actually involved two noncandidates. William Buckley, Jr., would speak from the right side of the spectrums and Gore Vidal would counter from the left. They made a good combo, Buckley and Vidal, and their interchange seemed unforced, lively, and appealingly acrimonious. I remember that because as a kid journalist, I was working not on the sports beat in those years, but as a TV critic, and ABC had provided me with an interview with Vidal on the morning that would lead to the night when the riots of Grant Park happened. That was the signature night of the entire 1960s when the Chicago cops, coached by Mayor Daley, would defeat the hippies—who were failed by their defensive coordinator, Abbie Hoffman—by a far greater margin than Mike Ditka's Chicago Bears would beat Raymond Berry's New England Patriots in the Windy City's only Super Bowl.

I complimented Vidal on the hostile edge that had insinuated itself into the debates and asked him if he and Buckley might not perhaps share some civil, if not cordial, moments when off camera. "No, not at all," I remember Vidal saying. "We genuinely hate each other's guts."

That became glaringly evident only a few hours later. In the process of exchanging verbal left jabs and right uppercuts, Vidal would use the term "crypto-Nazi" to characterize his opponent. To which Buckley spontaneously responded, in his finest intellectual-aristocratic clipped tonery, "Listen, you queer. You call me a Nazi and I'll bash your goddamn face in." Now that was climbing into unplowed land for network TV in those days (hell, now as well), and moderator Howard K. Smith admonished his debate duo for producing more "heat than light."

But that brief moment offered a hint of the raw energy that comes from honest and heartfelt confrontation. Roone Arledge recognized in that flash-point incident the quality that might make the difference for his *Monday Night Football*. Prime-time sports had been missing entirely from the networks since the death of Wednesday and Friday night boxing, and for team sports, Arledge's gambit was a first. A broadcast duo that offered not the hand-to-hand combat style of Buckley and Vidal but something snappily adversarial could be the one ingredient that would put the football experiment over the top.

What Arledge did perceive, back in the late sixties, was that the National Football League and network television were destined to become symbiotic entities, locked into a collision course that someday would morph into the entertainment industry cartel that presently exists. He realized that the standard-issue broadcast-booth personalities would soon become passé. Pro football was not a game anymore. It was pure showbiz, and it urgently required the narration of personalities who delivered a whole new category of bullshit to sustain the mass ratings that prime time so arduously demands.

Arledge, as sports broadcasting history will long note, located the chemistry that he so ardently desired in the teaming of Dandy Don Meredith, the glib and wisecracking former quarterback country boy, and Howard Cosell, the abrasive one, who used to like to say, "Marconi invented the microphone, but I showed people how to use it."

The plan was working nicely at midseason 1970. By the end of the year, the football telecasts would trail only *The Flip Wilson Show* and *The Mary Tyler Moore Show* in prime-time ratings, and by 1972, they would cause the cancellation of their main competition over at CBS, *Mayberry RFD*. ABC's Monday night cameras arrived in Dallas near midseason 1970 to telecast the game between the Cowboys and the then St. Louis Cardinals. It had been arranged for me to interview the broadcasters—one of them, at least—after they hit town on Sunday afternoon. Meredith, then as now, would not deign to participate in any media activity. That was something that the general public did not know about Dandy Don—beyond the range of the cameras, Meredith was not the joyous, convivial, happy-go-lucky sort who so effectively wore the white hat while Cosell took on the natural role of the loudmouthed and opinionated heavy.

At some point during the end of his playing career with the Dallas Cowboys—he retired after the Cowboys had been all but disintegrated by the Cleveland Browns in a calamitous playoff defeat after the 1968 season—Dandy Don was anything but dandy. He had become a sullen character and, according to rumors, embittered by an off-the-field event in his life that left him with the darkest lingering sentiments of all things Dallas.

That persists to this very day. Late in 1999, when it became apparent that Tom Landry would not overcome his battle with leukemia and was shortly to die, I was assigned to write a magazine requiem to the great coach, the most admired man who ever graced the streets of Dallas. I interviewed Roger Staubach. I interviewed Tex Schramm. I interviewed Mike Ditka. I interviewed Ernie Stautner—among others—and each and every one was generous with his time and comments.

Through a friend in Austin who knew Meredith's daughter, I was able to obtain Dandy Don's phone number. Meredith has been living in semiexile in Santa Fe for years. That's Santa Fe, as in New Mexico, a community occupied by well-to-do and self-appointed cloud critics—a large assembly of ponytailed poofters who like to dress up like the Cisco Kid.

On a weeknight, I called Meredith's house. His wife answered. A social event of some sort, judging from the faint background sounds of tinkling ice cubes and self-satisfied laughter, was taking place. I told Meredith's wife who I was and who employed me, and wondered if Dandy might spare a moment of his time to offer a recollection or two about his dying coach.

"Who gave you this phone number?" the woman demanded. I declined to answer at first, but when it became evident that she wouldn't turn the phone over to Meredith until she received an answer, I identified my contact. "Well, I'll cut *his* balls off," she said, although there was levity in her tone. She asked for my phone number. Given the circumstances of Landry's impending passing, Don, she said, might call me back the next morning. He didn't. Nor the following morning nor the next. The call I did receive was one from my friend in Austin, who informed me that Meredith's daughter had called to cuss him out and told him never to give out the number again.

So I never talked to Meredith in late 1999, any more than I did in his rookie broadcast year of 1970. The person ABC would provide me was Howard Cosell. (Keith Jackson was the third man in the booth that first season.) We met in the bar of the Fairmont Hotel in Dallas and drank scotch for three and a half hours. Cosell was taller than you might expect, far more gregarious than anybody would guess, and, boy, could he pack away the Chivas and soda. Around dusk, the interview ended. The plan then was that Jim Pratt, who worked in promotions for Channel 8, the Dallas ABC affiliate, would drive Cosell to a radio station in Highland Park where he would tape his syndicated radio program, drive me over to Love Field where I would fly to New Orleans to interview Ann Margret (holy shit, were those the days?), and then drive back to get Cosell and deliver him back to the Fairmont.

En route to the radio station, Pratt, who'd had a cocktail or two himself, managed to rear-end, ever so slightly, a Cadillac stopped at a red light on Preston Road. Pratt and the driver of the Caddy, an older guy, stepped out of the cars to survey the damage, if any. After about two minutes of this, Cosell suddenly transformed himself into his on-the-air personality. "Let's get this goddamn show on the road!" he yelled, and jumped out of Pratt's car. There were some raised voices outside that I couldn't quite hear, and suddenly we were en route to the station again. After dropping Cosell off, Jim Pratt shook his head and revealed the details of the street incident.

As Cosell had aggressively insisted that it was time to move on, an elderly woman on the passenger side of the Cadillac had said, "My goodness! It's that annoying man on the football games!" At which point Humble Howard provided the old lady with what had to be a moment she would never forget. Cosell leaned inside the Cadillac, pressed his face into hers, and shouted, "Fuck you!"

Atta boy, Howard.

Ancient scribes—and I must include myself among the surviving membership of that peat moss–encrusted lodge—sit around the campfire and talk still of what happened the next night on the Cowboys' world premiere on *Monday Night Football*. Even though the Cowboys would eventually not only rebound but advance to their first ever Super Bowl appearance, the Cardinals would stomp the bejesus out of Dallas, 38–0. The restive Cotton Bowl throng, realizing who was sitting in the broadcast booth, the football retiree they'd been booing since the inception of the franchise, started a chant. As the game got worse, the chant grew ever louder: "We want Meredith! We want Meredith!" On TV,

Meredith would finally respond, "They might want me, but I ain't coming."

Thanks to Howard's performance on Preston Road the night before, I'll always remember *Monday Night Football* in Dallas for an entirely different reason. Too bad nobody has any video footage of that reality show.

W hen Bill Parcells's Dallas Cowboys ventured to New York for a Monday night engagement to play the Giants in Week 2 of the 2003 season, the program had experienced many faces and voices in its presentation since that occasion I remembered so vividly, that night when Cosell had flipped out in 1970.

Frank Gifford. Dan Dierdorf. Boomer Esiason. Dan Fouts. Alex Karras. O. J. Simpson. Dennis Miller. Joe Namath. Fred "the Hammer" Williamson. They'd come. They'd gone. Now the show belonged to John Madden and Al Michaels.

Throughout the history of the *Monday Night* telecasts, four of its Top 10–rated games had involved the Dallas Cowboys, but none of them had been played recently. During the final season of the Campo tenure, the Cowboys were not included on the Monday night roster at all. They were appearing this time only because of the hype that might be stirred up over the Tuna returning to New York. The Tuna, in fact, was involved with the top-rated Monday night game ever. That was when his Giants played the 49ers in December of the 1990 season. Parcells's team lost that one but came back in a month to win the more vital rematch in the NFC championship game.

Throughout the week, Parcells claimed that he couldn't comprehend why anybody would care. After all, he'd come back plenty of times previously.

The last time he'd faced the Giants had been toward the end of that 1999 season with the Jets and the entire event was something that Big Bill would have chosen to erase from his memory bank. Jim Fassel's team had blistered the Jets, 41–21, and according to Parcells, "We played like a bunch of dogs. I can't describe our game with the Giants any better than that. They kicked our ass every way possible. Our defense in that game simply sucked. It couldn't have played out any worse than it did. That wasn't the greatest offense in the world we were playing against, either. I told the team in the locker room after the game that I was ashamed. Ashamed of myself as a coach and ashamed of them and their performance. There wasn't anyone on our side that could walk out of the locker room with their head held up. How could they?"

As far as the game against the Giants, ABC's promo people were underjoyed. This was one that should be out of doubt by halftime. Potential viewers would be turning to the History Channel for more stimulating forms of video thrills. Jim Fassel's team had overwhelmed the St. Louis Rams in every category of play in their opener. They kicked the Rams all over the field, 23–13, in a win keyed by a 77-yard completion from Kerry Collins to Amani Toomer. Tiki Barber had rushed for 146 yards against the Rams, and now the Cowboys somehow needed to put a stop to that with a defensive tackle combo that featured Willie Blade, who might not play with a gimped-up knee, and his more highly regarded partner, La'Roi Glover, who had recorded exactly one tackle against the Atlanta Falcons in the 27–13 opening-game defeat.

Dallas? Well, Tuna or no Tuna, the Cowboys had produced a lame second-half effort against the Falcons and there was no reason to suggest that would not persist into Week 2. Recent history, or the previous four seasons, at least, had seen Dallas post a 5–27 record on the road. What a nightmare this ought to be. Fullback Richie Anderson, trying not to appear tense, tied his shoes before the final workout that preceded the trip to New York. "Coach talks about punchin' back when you get punched," Anderson said. "That's called resiliency. We need a little of that. That's an identity we're trying to establish around here." The expression on Anderson's face indicated that he had no genuine notion as to what game, what month, what decade, such an identity might be restored to the Dallas Cowboys.

Which was why the Tuna, at the conclusion of his team's week of preparation, seemed so absolutely benign. Parcells, as the trip back to what the media had been attempting to trumpet as a homecoming was looming, seemed as content as he'd been since his arrival in Texas. He'd just delivered a message to his team. Chill, fellas. "Sometimes . . . I'd like to think . . . that my team is going to relax a little bit," he said afterward, although he had to agree that given the challenge, their apprehensions might be founded in reality.

"Well, we're going up to play against what might be the flagship franchise in the whole history of the NFL. And after losing last week, we're playing a stronger opponent this week. Also in a different and more challenging environment. This is Monday night, on the road. That's as hard as it can get, so I guess it's human nature to be . . ." He didn't finish the sentence but rather started a new one. "So I view this as a good opportunity."

Parcells said that after one official regular-season week on the job, he'd noticed something about the Cowboys' media folks and the fans as a group. "Here in Texas, everybody seems to become an instant evaluator," the Tuna said. In other words, the world around Parcells, in his estimation, had been overreacting to the Atlanta loss. "In three weeks, people will be picking the teams that are going to the Super Bowl. And in six weeks, they'll take it all back."

His biggest concern going into the Monday night Meadowlands maelstrom? That was easy. Quincy Carter. "I'll be interested to see his game management . . . his judgment under duress."

It didn't take long to find out. After trading punts, the Cowboys took the ball for their second possession, and on the first play, Carter retreated, threw to his right, and hit a wide-open Ralph Brown, who, unfortunately for Carter, played in the defensive backfield for the New York Giants. Brown strolled twenty-nine untouched yards into the Dallas end zone. On the sideline, the Tuna, who'd visited Bischoff's ice cream parlor in Teaneck with some of his former Giants players about four hours before the game, bit his lower lip but otherwise appeared serene, while, just as the ABC people had feared, the History Channel ratings enjoyed a sudden surge in the North Texas TV ratings.

But the ones who stayed to watch the carnage began to see something else. For the first time, Cowboys fans would witness the Tuna's mojo starting to kick in. That "they punch you, you punch them back" identity that Richie Anderson had spoken of so wistfully suddenly came into play. After Zuriel Smith returned a Giants punt thirty-seven yards, Carter quickly guided his team to the tying touchdown, one that he scored himself on an eight-yard dash through a gap of daylight that appeared in the Giants' red-zone defense.

Strangely, at least it was strange from the outlook of what Dallas fans had observed in recent years, the Cowboys threw the next punch, as well. Greg Ellis knocked the football out of Tiki Barber's grasp, Dat Nguyen recovered it, and Billy Cundiff, the man marked as Most Likely to Leave Town after his lamentable performance against the Falcons a week earlier, added a thirty-seven-yard field goal. Later in the quarter, Cundiff kicked another one, this time from forty-nine yards, and on the first play after the kickoff, Kerry Collins's intended pass to Jeremy Shockey—he of the homo quote—was speared by Al Singleton, the Dallas linebacker, who carried the ball back forty-one yards for a TD.

Dallas led at the half, 20–7, then dominated the third quarter as well. When Cundiff scored his fifth field goal of the game with 12:43 to play in the last quarter, the fans back home settled back to watch their team blow the game, just as it always had under Dave Campo. Later, Parcells would offer a review of his team's defensive effort for the remainder of the fourth quarter as "helter-skelter." That description was fitting enough in a macabre sense, since it was on a *Monday Night Football* game in 1980 that Howard Cosell first told the nation that John Lennon had been shot dead.

So, indeed, did it appear the Cowboys were headed for the same destiny. The team collapsed, utterly and completely, and it was only a natural progression of God's plan for the Cowboys' universe that Matt Bryant kicked a thirty-yard field goal that gave New York the lead, 32–29, with eleven lousy, stinking seconds to play. Had coach Jim Fassel chosen to run one more play, that kick would have happened with one second to play, instead of eleven. Fassel would later opine that the option of running the clock down to nothing hadn't seemed like such a big deal at the time.

Funny how things in life can change so suddenly. After the commercials, Matt Bryant, kicker of the apparently winning field goal, was suddenly transformed into Matt Bryant, what the fuck were you thinking? Bryant's kickoff was deep but angled too sharply toward the coffin corner of the end zone. Zuriel Smith, the Dallas rookie man, had been a sixth-round draft choice from Hampton and came to Texas with a scouting report with such notations as "quick, elusive ball handler who breaks the long one with great footwork and a burst of speed . . . not strong and has difficulty getting out of jams at the line of scrimmage . . . more quick than fast . . . his return abilities make him an intriguing prospect."

What the scouting reports did not say was "has an amazing capacity to stand and do nothing while the Giants' special team thunders down his throat and the *Monday Night Football* world watches, and allows the kickoff to bounce out-of-bounds not a yard and a half shy of the end zone, giving his team one last op-portunity to tie the game." Parcells shrugged it off. "Things don't seem to bother him much. I don't know why," Parcells conceded. "Maybe he just doesn't understand it yet."

Thus, the Cowboys got the ball at their own forty-yard line, with those same eleven precious seconds still remaining on the clock. The following day, Parcells's old pal Bobby Knight, of all people, would phone him to rave about Smith's demonstration of amazing cool under fire. Now Quincy Carter, the man who'd worn the "Can't Play" sandwich-board sign since the day he had arrived in Dallas, was challenged with running the Cowboys' eleven-second offense. He had one chance.

It was the Tuna who called the play. Dallas lined up in a shotgun formation, with three receivers bunched on the right side, Antonio Bryant alone on the left. With the Giants playing a zone, nobody was available to put a jam on Bryant at the scrimmage line, giving him a chance to sprint downfield and cut open toward the sideline. Carter fired a twenty-six-yard frozen rope to his receiver—a twenty-five-yarder might have left Cundiff beyond his range—and Bryant caught the ball as he tiptoed out-of-bounds. Cundiff, who was still on the team only because Parcells perhaps could not locate anybody on the waiver wire after the Atlanta game, delivered the kick, a fifty-two-yarder, when the Tuna punched his right fist toward the sky.

Cundiff's twenty-five-yarder, his seventh of the game and the one that would win it once and for all in overtime, served as nothing but an anticlimax. The game winner, a tap-in compared with the kick that had sent this amazing game into overtime, was set up on a twenty-three-yard completion to tight end Dan Campbell. This was Campbell, the ex-Giant who'd been recommended to Parcells by offensive assistant coach Sean Payton, the coach who'd essentially been let go by the Giants the previous season. This was a night that was crammed with irony.

"It [the fifty-two-yard stunner that tied the game] doesn't really mean much right now," Cundiff would say after the game, and then offer a qualifying appendage. "I'll probably tell my children about it someday." As for Carter, the man who'd entered training camp as the scatter-armed pariah, he'd finished the game with 321 passing yards, and that early interception that had seemed to doom the Cowboys, the one that Ralph Brown had taken to the house, would be Carter's only pickoff among the forty passes he attempted. In the process, Carter substantially outplayed his counterpart, Kerry Collins.

This Week 2 showpiece would remain branded upon the hindquarters of both contestants for the remainder of the season. Clearly, this was the occasion that catapulted Dallas into its astonishing playoff run. As for the other team, Giants coach Jim Fassel would be seeking another job at the end of the season.

The following day back at Valley Ranch, Bill Parcells would allow his team to run, lift some weights, and take the rest of the day off. He wasn't doing that out of charity necessarily. The upcoming weekend would be the Cowboys' bye week. His assessment of the team's win, the game that would turn the season completely around? "I've seen the film, and I'm not naming names, but we had four or five guys who didn't show up. Oh, they appeared in the game, all right, but they didn't do anything. I'll be talking to them later in the week."

CHAPTER 13

"A DIAMOND AMONG TRASH," OR HOW TO PISS OFF YOUR FRIENDS

Among the many proud statistical categories in which Texas annually leads the other forty-nine states is the percentage of native-born citizens who go to hell when they die. Texas took the top spot away from California sometime during the early to mid-1950s, right about the time Lyndon Johnson started usurping vast elements of power in the U.S. Senate.

And despite what outsiders might hear about what July and August are like around here, it's September that genuinely serves most Texans as a prep school for the afterlife. Vague hints of autumn tend to appear in the air after Labor Day in other parts of the land. September in Texas offers no relief. The summer death march just seems to stagger ever onward. There is no evidence of eventual reprieve. Urban areas suffer most. Because the grass and trees of a circle of countryside bisected by 120-mile diameters were long ago bulldozed and paved, the ever-relentless heat reflects off the concrete and asphalt surfaces to inflict a tyranny of ultimate outdoor discomfort. These are the times that fry men's souls.

As the Dallas Cowboys football players arrived at a well-guarded remote parking area of D-FW Airport, the chartered American Airlines jet sitting beyond the chain-link fence out on the runway was the most welcome of sights. The Saturday flight to New Jersey for the Sunday game against the Jets would provide more than a quick escape from the spirit-deflating September sunshine. A football game gave the players a furlough from the practice sessions that had been conducted by the wicked coach Parcells. Because of an oddly scheduled Week 3 bye, the team had been exposed to two solid weeks of uninterrupted badgering from their foul-mouthed czar.

Parcells had let each individual on the team realize what they were in for when he first got to Texas. "If you're sensitive, you're gonna have a hard time around here. I have a bad temper—I swear. I yell. I do a lot of things. If you're not sensitive, you'll get along just fine." Ever the person to immerse himself in detail, Parcells was certain that every player had received and understood that message before he ever set foot in the weight room or practice field.

The two weeks that followed the Giants game, from the players' aspect, had been like a tooth extraction without laughing gas. Had they not prevailed in the cliff-hanger finish on Monday night and produced the comeback win that rivaled the Hail Mary days of the Tom Landry Age, Parcells's approach would have been less severe. They'd won, though, and the Tuna now had a foundation to build a season around. So there would be no mint tea and Godiva chocolates being served on the practice field.

The Cowboys entourage boarded the plane. Parcells and Jerry Jones occupied the two seats, left aisle, at the front of first class. Jerry's son Stephen and the rest of the coaching staff filled out the first-class seating. Media people used to travel on the charter flights and sit up front, but that practice had been abandoned during the mid-1980s, mandated by the people who run the media offices as initiated by their hypocritical and chickenshit no-conflict-of-interest ethics kick.

Various team support staff and front-office minions filled the seats of the first rows of tourist seating and, beyond them, the players, with an empty seat between each of them on both sides of the aisle all the way to the back of the plane. That was the standard seating arrangement with not only the Cowboys but all NFL teams, and had been forever. Under Parcells, one change had been put into place. On the return trips, the beverage carts in the back of the plane would contain no alcohol.

Cowboys charters were always scheduled to arrive the afternoon before the game, between 4:00 and 5:00 P.M., local time. A bus then carried the players to the hotel. For the Jets game, that would be the Jersey City Hyatt Regency. For the Giants game two weeks earlier, the team had been quartered at the Hasbrouck Hilton. Upon arrival, the players divided into two groups, offense and defense, and attended pregame meetings. These were an exercise in redundancy. After their careers are over, the reality sinks in upon the professional football players. All those meetings are conducted for the sole purpose of fund-raising, since the fines for falling asleep in those sessions are conventionally substantial.

Then comes mealtime. In the past, this was a team function held in a hotel banquet room. Under Parcells, that had changed as well. The Tuna's policy is to give each player an envelope containing cash, and the player can eat anywhere in town he chooses, with the one exception of the hotel bar. Most simply opt for room service.

The Jets fans who piled into the Meadowlands were less worshipful of Bill Parcells than the Giants faithful that had preceded them in the Monday night game. The Giants remembered the two Super Bowl championships he'd brought home. Jets faithful—some of them—fostered a resentment toward the Tuna for quitting on them before earning the ultimate prize. And they were impatient, too, after an 0–2 start. They got loud early when the Jets, featuring the Tuna's prize pupil from the past, Curtis Martin, started running the ball.

New York took a 3–0 lead and it appeared that might begin to snowball. Then Dallas started doing things Tuna style. Eric Ogbogu, a player Parcells had added to his roster for defensive-line depth after Dallas seemed to have worn down in the second half of the opener against Atlanta, knocked the football loose from Santana Moss and the Cowboys had a turnover near midfield. Shortly, they took the lead for good when Troy Hambrick ran through a massive hole opened by the right side of the Dallas line. For once, Hambrick did not fall on his face eight yards down the field, as he would whenever he got into the secondary for almost all of the remainder of the season, and scored from thirty-one yards. Ogbogu had been on the Jets' roster under Parcells and had been cut. "Class clown," Parcells remembered. "And now he's married to a schoolteacher and has grown up."

With less than two minutes left in the half, the 20 percent "high achiever" club that Parcells preordains as players who usually produce the key elements of almost every win would offer an illustration of why that theory works. Vinnie Testaverde, subbing for the wounded Chad Pennington, rifled back-to-back passes that carried from the Jets' thirty-two to the Cowboys' twenty. Then Curtis Martin squirted past the Dallas line and was seemingly touchdown-bound when Roy Williams—the same player viewed by Parcells as the young Ronnie Lott—stripped the ball out of Martin's grip at the eleven-yard line. The ball bounced forward into the end zone, where the Tuna's other star safety, Darren Woodson, recovered it for a touchback. Dallas hustled the ball down to the Jets' thirteen and made a stab at the end zone. Bryant caught Quincy Carter's pass at the back of the end zone. The back judge ruled Bryant out-of-bounds. Parcells challenged, and the TV replay proved him right. For the second straight game, Dallas would take a double-digit lead into the Meadowlands locker. This time, Dallas wouldn't require any of those Hail Mary dramatics that are the kind of thing that might land the Tuna back into cardiac post-op. Dallas won, 17–6. The postgame stats provided something of interest to Parcells.

In training camp, he'd looked at his linebacker corps, led by veterans Dat Nguyen and Dexter Coakley, and noted that they bore little resemblance, stature-wise, to the Lawrence Taylor–Carl Banks prototype. He said, "Actually, they remind me of those clowns they stuff into the little cars at the circus."

Against the Jets, this Nguyen-Coakley duo, the ones that Parcells had mistaken for extras in a Judy Garland movie, had been the principal factor that kept the Jets out of the Dallas end zone.

They'd combined for twelve solo tackles and six assists. So now a football team with undersized defenders and an overaged coach was on something of a roll.

Emmitt Smith, the exemplary warrior, was the player that Jerry Jones most had to thank for those three Lombardi Trophies that glistened at Valley Ranch. In deference to Troy Aikman and Michael Irvin, they had been the guys who had gotten to the fun stuff, playing catch out in the open field. Well, okay, maybe it wasn't always a backseat-after-the-senior-prom experience for the latter two, since Aikman can no longer remember his name on frequent occasions, and one Sunday, Irvin was carried off the field in Philadelphia with no feeling in his body from the chin down and never played again. But it was Emmitt Smith who slugged it out down in the coal pits game in and game out, supplying the grit and the backbone for the Dallas offense.

In 2003 Smith would become the galvanizing force that would lead the Cowboys on yet another playoff drive, the most unlikely one in their history. Interestingly, he inspired an entire Dallas team while wearing the uniform of the Arizona Cardinals. In an interview that appeared in *Sports Illustrated* in early August, Smith had told the magazine's pro football expert, Peter King, that in his final season in Dallas he, Smith, had been "a diamond among trash."

When the magazine hit the nation's newsstands and mailboxes, the Cowboys were in the early phase of two-a-day toil in San Antonio—a team with a new coach, a recent history of losing and losing big, and no identity. Smith's remark—and it wasn't the diamond part that pissed the players off so badly—unified the team. Very suddenly, this lost-in-the-forest football team had been equipped with a purpose. Trash? *Au contraire.*

As the players left the practice field after a morning workout, reporters hit them with a cascade of questions regarding the infamous Emmitt quote. By then, the players had been well-coached in the Bill Parcells School of How to Deal with the Media—"those guys [reporters] are not your friends, even though they might act like they are. Limit your responses to 'I am just trying to make a contribution to the team,' and nothing more, no matter what the question is. Always be suspicious"— and so Emmitt's former teammates supplied the standard-issue Cream of Wheat statements regarding the magazine business. Parcells himself had his pat answer: "I didn't hear him say it, so I can't comment."

Charlie Waters, the ex-Cowboy, was still in San Antonio preparing for some pregame radio stints when the Smith stuff hit. Since Waters was not bound by the modern-league protocols against telling the truth, he offered this take on what had taken place and what was to come: "When Arizona comes to Dallas, they [the Dallas players] are going to tear Emmitt's fucking head off." Waters was laughing when he said that.

Now, the long-awaited Game 4 of the regular season against the Cardinals was at hand. Emmitt Smith was returning to the scene of his former glories, Texas Stadium. This also had been the site, not quite a year before, that Smith had broken Walter Payton's career rushing record. The Cowboys' whole marketing approach for the 2002 campaign had been based around Smith's pursuit of Payton's yardage totals. Imagine. An NFL football team gearing its entire season around an individual player's *stat.*

And really, it wasn't that historically significant a stat as far as stats go. Not like, say, somebody going after Joe DiMaggio's fifty-six-game hitting streak. When Smith finally reached the mark against Seattle, the game was stopped to commemorate the occasion, and you'd have thought Mel Gibson had descended through the hole of the Texas Stadium roof, riding his cross like a Harley. Trumpets blared. Thousands of balloons were unleashed. The show included everything but the Three Tenors—Pavarotti, Carreras, and Domingo—marching onto the field and singing "Ave Maria." For a minute, I thought Bert Parks would come out and give number 22 a bouquet of roses. Man, I've seen classier displays of pomp and circumstance at the Miss Port-a-Can Pageant in Ponca City, Oklahoma. That part of it wasn't Emmitt's fault. He hadn't planned the show. But the part where he ran over to his blocking buddy Daryl Johnston and wept on the Moose's shoulder right there on live TV—would somebody please pass the Pepto-Bismol? After the game resumed, Dallas went ahead and lost to Seattle, not that anybody gave a crap about technicalities like the final score in those pre-Tuna days.

Emmitt had not done too much in his return to Dallas, but he looked nice. For such an abysmal football team, those Cardinals sure wear snappy-looking uniforms—next to the Cowboys, the best in the league, I think. Early in the second quarter, Smith had five carries for minus one yard. Any doubt that Smith had endowed his old team with serious focus had been erased with the sheer intensity of the manner that the defense went after him. What must have been gratifying to Bill Parcells and Mike Zimmer was, starting with the Giants game, even when somebody other than Emmitt had the ball, the defense seemed to pretend that it was Smith.

On Smith's sixth carry, Charlie Waters's prediction came to pass, to a certain extent. The Cowboys didn't tear Emmitt's fucking head off. But they broke his fucking shoulder. So that would be it for Smith, not only for this game but for most of the remainder of the season as well.

Dallas won the game easily, 24–7, in a showing that was highlighted when first La'Roi Glover and then Eric Ogbogu sacked Jeff Blake in his end zone for safeties on back-to-back possessions—a franchise first for the Dallas defense.

Late in the contest, Jason Witten, the Tuna's prize rookie, took a fluke helmet shot that landed beneath his face guard. Witten's jaw was broken, and he crawled to the Dallas bench on his hands and knees, spitting out blood and teeth. Parcells was not unaware of Witten's plight.

After the game was over, Parcells addressed his football players. "Great effort, guys!" he yelled. "Witten! Lead us in three cheers!"

In a pregame ceremony at Texas Stadium, Jerry Jones paid homage to a figure from those thrilling days of Cowboys' yesteryear, Tex Schramm. Dallas's GM from the outset of the franchise, Schramm had been credited with inventing, or at least suggesting, everything new in the modern-day National Football League except Howard Cosell's toupee. Schramm was to be inducted into the Cowboys' Ring of Honor, an exclusive society of former players and one coach that is more notable for who is not in it than who is.

It was Tex Schramm who designed those satin silver-and-blue

Cowboys uniforms. It was also Tex who encouraged a makeover of the cheerleaders on the Dallas sidelines. In the early years, those were wholesome high school kids moonlighting on Sundays. Tex wanted white boots, hot pants, and cleavage. It is probably not true that Tex had a two-way mirror installed in the cheerleaders' dressing room for his personal entertainment and certainly not true that it was Tom Landry's idea, but Tex never would deny it. That was the kind of guy Tex was.

I remember visiting Tex's house in late 1996 to talk about the infamous game that was played in Green Bay. The Packers won on the last play of the game, and everyone froze their nuts off. During our visit, Tex's wife, Marty, arrived at the house from some errands and entered through the back door. She had been in Green Bay that day, too, and Tex thought his wife could provide some insight as well. "Marty," he yelled. "Come in here and talk to this guy about the goddamn Ice Bowl game!"

Mrs. Schramm, a delicately featured woman with the bone structure of a Chihuahua puppy, patiently offered her recollections. "I was sitting with Alicia [Landry] in the stands and we were not dressed for the weather. Some Green Bay fans recognized who we were and gave us large plastic bags to wrap ourselves in; otherwise we might not have survived," she related. "By the fourth quarter, it had gotten so cold that whenever I got any moisture in my eyes, my eyes would literally freeze shut and I would have to pry the lids apart with my fingers."

Tex looked at Marty in mock amazement. "Well, how'd you take a leak?" he demanded.

Marty died in April 2003; Tex's death followed three months later. All of the surviving members of the Ring of Honor showed up for the ceremony—all save Don Meredith, of course, who apparently deemed the whole business rather beneath him.

Dandy should have made it into town, not just because of Tex's little ceremony but for a hell of a good football game. The Philadelphia Eagles were playing. Unlike the Cowboys, then at a startling 3–1, Philly was sputtering with a 2–2 record. Just as Emmitt Smith might have ignited something inside the Cowboys with his insult, the Eagles, too, had been put on notice from an unlikely source.

Rush Limbaugh had just been canned from his ESPN gig for stating that Donovan McNabb's star quarterback credentials were a product of the liberal media, in the left-wingers' desire to see the black quarterback succeed. Here's where Rush was off-base. Unlike the listeners who tune in to his radio program to obtain the whole scope of their political insight, NFL fans don't need the media, liberal or otherwise, to determine which players are worth a damn or not.

It hadn't been a very good week for Limbaugh. After his dismissal from ESPN, he was dragged into this mess about his housekeeper obtaining mass quantities of prescription painkillers. That particular medication, hydrocodone, listed constipation as a side effect, which might explain the content of Rush's radio show, but it's not for me to say. Limbaugh himself was about to admit that he was hooked, and then he wimped out and entered treatment. C'mon, Rush. Don't be such a wuss. Prescription painkillers addictive? Bullshit. I've been eating them like Cracker Jacks for forty years.

So if the Eagles weren't cocked and loaded coming into the Dallas game, McNabb was. The boys in green had every reason to feel good. They'd beaten Dallas in six straight games, none of them even remotely close. Before the game, the Philly coach, Andy Reid, decided to roll the dice. As mentioned earlier in this text, Reid had initiated the Dave Campo era by successfully attempting an onside kick to open the game.

Why not replicate the feat again, as an in-your-face tribute to Bill Parcells? Reid, who'd coached his Eagles to the lip of the Super Bowl cup the previous two seasons but hadn't quite sank the putt, seemed compelled to illustrate that there was one head-coaching genius at work in the NFC East, and it was damn sure that he didn't answer to the name of Tuna.

Terrible idea, Andy. Just awful. Remember how the Tuna had labored overtime to secure Bruce DeHaven as his special-teams coach? Just as the Dallas kickoff return team trotted onto the field to begin the game, DeHaven buttonholed one of his players, Randal Williams, who could run like an antelope. "Watch out for an onside kick," DeHaven told Williams.

David Akers pooch-kicked the ball perfectly—or it would have been perfect had the ball landed. Williams, racing forward, snatched the kick in midair and sprinted thirty-seven yards into the Philly end zone. From start to finish, the entire process lasted exactly three seconds. It was the fastest touchdown scored in an NFL game since the league began using the electronic clock in 1972. "He [DeHaven] didn't speak to anyone but me," Williams remembered later. "When I saw the kicker approach the ball, he took a bowed approach, and I thought something shady might be happening. I jumped up to catch the ball, and I thought I was going to get knocked out. Instead, I landed on both feet and saw nothing but green in front of me and thought, Why not?" All

Andy Reid could do was stand on the Eagles' sideline and look stupid.

Since Dallas wound up beating the Eagles, 23–21, the opening kickoff turned out to be a big play—and probably should be listed as in a dead heat with the final eleven seconds in the Monday night game against the Giants for what politicians like to call "the defining moment" of the Cowboys' season. Billy Cundiff, who had risen from the rank of pencil-necked geek to superstud, punctuated a Dallas comeback with a twenty-eight-yard field goal with 1:11 to go. The Eagles still had an opportunity to win it. They were near midfield with a whole minute left. On third-and-ten, Roy Williams and Dexter Coakley blitzed and sawed McNabb in half. The ball came loose and Coakley recovered it. Game over.

Afterward, the Tuna didn't have anything funny or poignant to say. That was perhaps because his team was now 4–1, with the remaining three teams in his division stuck in reverse. The Tuna could only be thinking, I'd told these jerks to elevate their expectations when I rolled in here. But this is getting out of hand.

Quincy, the quarterback who Bill Parcells had entrusted with driving his bus and directing his symphony, had been shifting gears and waving the baton like an impassioned man five games deep into the season. Parcells had informed his coaches that knowing Carter's love affair with the sport of baseball, he'd presented Quincy with a trivia question: Who was the only player in the history of major-league baseball who got traded for himself? "If you know, don't tell Quincy, because he's still trying to figure it out," Parcells was telling people. Now with things going so well, why would Parcells fuck with the kid's head like that? Oh well. It was his team.

The coach was pleased with Carter's overall play and happier yet with how he was adhering to the Tuna's ten-point list for quarterbacks. The ten items on that agenda were Parcells's secret, although point 1 was "Don't listen to anybody's advice on how to quarterback your team. Not the fans, not the media, not your wife or family, because nobody outside the locker room has the slightest notion as to what's going on." And point 10 was "I don't like celebrity quarterbacks."

Carter had been getting all kinds of off-the-field reminders ever since he'd arrived in Dallas, of course, so Bill's list was nothing new. It was Deion Sanders who had advised against buying a big house. "The more rooms you got," the Neon Man had told Carter, "the more people you got."

While Parcells had been strangely un-Tuna-like in his recently humane approach with the quarterback, he'd been characteristically unmerciful with other players. In the first practice after the Eagles game, when the players' noses were still being tickled by the champagne bubbles, Parcells took Darren Woodson aside. The message was harsh. While Darren Woodson will never make it into the NFL Hall of Fame, his credentials after eleven seasons in Dallas were beyond anybody's reproach.

Woodson was the franchise's all-time leading tackler, and every tackle he'd made had left the person with the football hearing air-raid sirens blaring in the back of his head. Now Parcells was berating him in a diatribe that offered charges ranging from treason to gutlessness. "When it comes down to it, this team still has a mind-set that they're a bunch of goddamn losers! It makes me sick," Parcells yelled.

What he was doing with Woodson—who found the entire incident amusing, although surprising—was simply to pass the message to the team, through his most reliable veteran player, that it was time to intensify their focus. The climb that lay ahead was about to grow steeper by the week, and the slopes would get icier. Parcells would concede that his session with Woodson might have been construed as "a little bit of a tantrum."

Now Dallas was transporting its 4–1 record to Detroit to play the 1–4 Lions. Ordinarily, there was room for optimism with this matchup, but the slogan from Dallas's standpoint had become "Motown Is No Town to Be In." By a scheduling quirk, nine of the previous ten Cowboys-Lions games had been played in Detroit, and the Lions almost always won, no matter how good the Cowboys had been. "We've never won in Detroit since I've owned the team," Jerry Jones pointed out. Jerry was mistaken. Dallas had beaten the Lions in the Silverdome, 37–3, in 1992 when the J-J corps won their first Super Bowl. But that was back when Jerry was still into martinis, so he probably forgot. Dallas sure as hell hadn't done anything up there lately, and Jones's 1994 team that *should* have won the Super Bowl had managed to lose to a crappy Detroit team in overtime.

Everything pointed to another dismal outing halfway through the first quarter, after Troy Hambrick lost a fumble and Dre Bly of the Lions scooped the football and ran it back sixty-two yards for a score. Then Aveion Cason fumbled the next kickoff, but the officials dug through a pile of players and ruled that Bradie James had recovered the ball for Dallas. "That recovery—right there—if we didn't get the ball, that might have killed us on the spot," Parcells said later.

After that Dallas took charge. Terry Glenn caught not one, not two, but three first-half TD balls from Carter. Then Dallas's corner Mario Edwards scored on a pickoff of Detroit's alleged second-year quarterback savior, Joey Harrington, who was about to be yanked. The Cowboys' halftime lead was 28–7, and while that was enough to carry to the bank, Parcells witnessed something at the start of the second half that he'll treasure among his eventual Dallas memories.

The Cowboys took the kickoff and drove eighty-one yards to eventually score a touchdown. The drive consumed fifteen plays; ten of them were runs. The march consumed half of the third-quarter clock.

Detroit's possession was a three-and-out that consumed one minute and one second. Dallas got the ball and kept it the remainder of the quarter, before Cundiff kicked a field goal on the first play of the last period.

"Anybody notice? We controlled the ball nearly fourteen minutes of the third quarter—on the road!" In Parcells's football galaxy, things get no better than that. And for the remainder of the season, they wouldn't.

CHAPTER 14

"WE'RE FLYING ON A BURNING PLANE"

It was fall of 2002 and I was examining the galley proofs for a story that I'd written for *Playboy* magazine, along with the full-page illustration that accompanied the article. That little rabbit's head logo appeared at the bottom of the last page.

Right then, my thirteen-year-old son walked into the room. "Look, here's my *Playboy* article," I told him.

"Well, I was watching Jay Leno last night," the kid announced, "and he said that reading the stories in *Playboy* was like going to Hooter's for the chicken wings."

Huh? Being a puritan father, I didn't tell him this, but a large percentage of *Playboy*'s circulation base will chronically ejaculate prematurely, so those guys have plenty of leftover time to read the stories. Evidently, that condition runs rampant on the Gulf Coast, where the whole population, after it had worked its way beyond the "Women of Starbucks" photo display, had read Bucs coach Jon Gruden's comments in the interview of the September issue of the magazine. That's their big football issue, in which Mike Holmgren was named coach of the "all-overpaid team." Somebody wrote, "Holmgren was brought to Seattle to turn the team around, and all he has done is give local deejays a reason to play 'I Am the Walrus.'"

Gruden was the Brad Pitt of the NFL coaching ranks, which apparently was deemed just cause for his selection to participate in the *Playboy* interview, where individuals like Martin Luther King, Muhammad Ali, and Bill Gates had come before him. It was in a *Playboy* interview that President Jimmy Carter owned up to having lust in his heart. That was the largest-selling issue in the history of the magazine.

Gruden had done his best to one-up Jimmy. He talked about the joy that comes with coaching a Super Bowl winner and said that if the Bucs did it again, he'd "dance in a jockey strap on the Dale Mabry Freeway."

Some of Gruden's comments were not football related.

Question: "How did you learn about sex?"

Gruden: "I had a big brother. I had friends. I liked girls at a young age, and I explored. I was like Christopher Columbus, finding a New World."

So Christopher Columbus crossed the ocean blue in 1492 just to get laid? Makes sense.

Lest Jon Gruden become too overwhelmed with his celebrity status, I might temper it some with this news flash. Since I have strong connections with the internal brass at *Playboy* (Hef and I have been tight for years), I can confirm that Bill Parcells was approached first for that interview and declined. (It should also be remembered that Gruden had been hired at Tampa, with its prepackaged Super Bowl roster, only after Parcells had turned that job down, too.) Since Parcells was all-consumed with the heartbreakingly awesome challenge of towing the Dallas Cowboys out of the mire of their ditch, the distraction that might come from providing his innermost thoughts to a stroke book was hardly worth the time.

Good choice, apparently, since Dallas was now 5–1 and seemingly living in a script that had been crafted by Rod Serling. Parcells refused to concede that his team was adrift in a twilight zone, but that was all a load of the usual horse crap that the Tuna so loves to dump upon the media during times of prosperity. "Coach, before the start of the season, if somebody had offered you a five–one record at this point, would you have taken it?"

"No," Parcells said, attempting to look and sound almost angelic. "That would have meant conceding that we would lose a game, and I never do that."

Down in Tampa, the Bucs were struggling, as most defending Super Bowl champs do in the "new" NFL, with its roller-coaster parity concept now in full force. The Bucs were stuck in neutral with a 3–3 record, and the prospect of Jon Gruden performing any jockey-strap cha-cha dances on the freeway was remote. What, though, of the notion that Bill Parcells might be engaging in a dance of his own after the next Super Bowl? That 5–1 record was enough to induce all kinds of hallucinations, all of a sudden. Thanks to the generosity of President Bush's tax cuts, the plutocracy of the Dallas area could once again afford the finest glue on the market, and that's what they had been inhaling all too deeply, according to some of the callers who expressed their views on all three of the D-FW market radio stations that were exclusively patterned to the sports-talk format.

Really, that 5–1 mark that was printed in black-and-white in the football standings in the sports pages—and the newspapers never lie, do they?—had been the wildest illusion of them all. After the Cowboys' trip to Florida, peace and sanity would be restored to the North Texas asylum. Warren Sapp and the rest of the Bucs defense exposed the Dallas offense for what Parcells had feared it had been all along.

Quincy Carter pitched a shutout, and the Bucs won, 16–0. A play in the second quarter turned the game around, and Parcells's stomach along with it. With Dallas down 3–0, the Bucs drove into the Dallas red zone. A third-and-five pass from Brad Johnson to Keenan McCardell at the Cowboys' fourteen had fallen incomplete, and now Martin Gramatica kicked the field goal that elevated the Bucs' lead to 6 points. Dallas was still in the game. But Terrence Newman, the prize rookie cornerback, slid into Gramatica's leg during the follow-through on the kick and out came the yellow flag. Gruden opted to remove the 3 points from the scoreboard and take the first down, and two plays later, Johnson threw the seven-yard touchdown pass to Keyshawn Johnson. *Ka-bam.* Now it was 10–nil, as the soccer people say, and that's appropriate, because in a defensive show like this one, it might as well have been a World Cup match. When you're behind by more than one score with a "nil" tacked to your scoreboard, there ain't gonna be no comeback.

The more galling aspect of the entire misadventure in Tampa, from the Tuna's outlook, came on four big plays when Dallas had the ball:

FIRST QUARTER

Ball at the Dallas thirty-three, third down and one: Troy Hambrick up the middle for a one-yard loss.

Ball at the Tampa twenty-two, third down and one: Troy Hambrick up the middle for a one-yard loss.

SECOND QUARTER

Ball at the Dallas forty-eight, third down and one: Richie Anderson catches Quincy Carter's pass and is run out-of-bounds for a two-yard loss.

FOURTH QUARTER

Ball at the Dallas twenty-four, third down and one: Richie Anderson up the middle, no gain.

Oh-for-four on third-and-one. "It's ridiculous," Parcells said. "We ought to be able to make a foot or a yard, but we weren't aggressive enough on the offensive line."

With Dallas's onetime archrival, the Washington Redskins, arriving at Texas Stadium, I was interested in the mood of the Cowboys players. Ever since they'd beaten the Giants in Week 2, it seemed that every game from then on had become a crossroads event, if not a crisis. Dallas, even after the wreckage in Tampa, still stood tall at 5–2. The 'Skins were 3–4 and apparently sinking fast. What a spot for an ambush. So what was lurking in the minds of the Cowboys players? Worry? Confident aggression? What?

After spending forty-five minutes with them in the locker room at midweek, I learned one thing for certain, and that was that the insightful reporter wouldn't learn a fucking thing about these players' actual thoughts, because the Tuna's media clampdown was so firmly in place. Here's the setup. Reporters, be they print, radio, or TV, have access to the locker room for that mandated forty-five minutes. But—and here's a substantial but—the players who do not wish to meet with reporters can hide in the trainer's room, which is off-limits to the media, and that's where the vast majority of them retreat when the media arrive.

The ones who don't will not say a damn thing worth hearing, anyway. Not that the broadcast people care. They're only in there to capture the less-than-three-second sound bite. It doesn't matter how meaningless, how mundane, how clichéd. As long as some jock says it, it's enough to put on the air. And that's another complaint. Where, all of a sudden, did all these radio-TV assholes come from to begin with? Not to mention all of the women, who, despite the bullshit that you hear from them, are in there to see if it's true about the size of these black dudes' cocks. And don't think the gals don't get off on it, 'cause they do, and the black guys, at least the ones who've got something to show off—and not all of them do—they don't mind a damn bit either.

Back in my day, when players like Johnny U. and Jim Brown were still in the game, and all of the players chain-smoked before and after the game, the locker-room scene was for the newspaper guys, and I emphasize *guys*, only. Now the territory has been completely taken over by the electronic media, just like Alcoholics Anonymous, where all the heroin addicts rule the sessions. And just as the TV journalists regard the newspaper people, the opium junkies look down their noses at the alkies and regard them as second-class addicts.

So I arrived at the Redskins game Sunday not knowing what to expect from the team. This was an early November afternoon, the temperature was eighty and the humidity was 70 percent. The pregame ceremony was an ironic affair. The Cowboys paid tribute to their longtime radio play-by-play announcer, Brad Sham, which was appropriate. While ratings in this category are not available, I would wager that the Dallas broadcast market leads the NFL by far in the number of households in which the TV audio is turned off so the people can listen to Sham and his color guy, ex-quarterback Babe Laufenberg. (Author's digression: Most discerning football fans also turn off the video portion of the NFL televised games since the cretins at the Fox Network started employing that camera-on-cable, a leftover novelty from the glory days of the XFL. That shows the play from above and behind the offensive backfield, the same view fans get from the stands in the end-zone sections at the stadium, where you can't see anything. Don't those fucking idiots at Fox realize that's why they call them the cheap seats?)

The beauty of the presentation to honor Sham was that not a decade ago, Sham had called Jerry Jones a liar on one of his broadcasts, and Jones fired him.

Then—after listening to a guy named Dave Barnett attempting to replicate Sham's style and doing it in a manner that was about as stimulating as eating homemade Sheetrock ice cream— Jones brought Sham back.

For Cowboys fans, the pregame activities were more stimulating than the game itself. If Dallas's preseason exhibition in Arizona had been a dog's lunch, in Parcells's estimation, then the first quarter and a half against the Redskins was what the dog coughed up after the meal proved indigestible. The horror show would proceed as follows.

- Derek Ross, a cornerback with an erratic history under Parcells, had been inserted as a kickoff return man. Ross made the most of the assignment, taking the opening kickoff and running it back one hundred yards, only to see his heroics nullified by a holding call.

- After the penalty, on Dallas's second play from scrimmage, Carter threw a deep ball to Joey Galloway that was intercepted by the Redskins.

- Dallas held, got the ball back, and on first down, Troy Hambrick fumbled, and the 'Skins got it again. In exactly two minutes and thirty-one seconds, the Cowboys had already made enough mistakes to screw up two games. They weren't through either.

- After Dallas's defense held again, Carter would promptly throw his second interception, this one being returned back to the Cowboys' six-yard line. Now this time, Washington would score. Flozell Adams blocked the extra point, and after such an outlandish start, it was stranger yet that Dallas trailed only 6–zip, which beat the hell out of 6–nil, which the score would have been had the Cowboys been playing a team that was any good.

- When Dallas regained the ball and began to drive, Carter rocketed a perfect shot to Terry Glenn for a thirty-five-yard touchdown, and—wait. What's that on the field? Why, it's a yellow handkerchief. Tight end Jason Witten, back in the lineup after recovering from the busted jaw he'd sustained in the

Cardinals game, had been flagged for illegal motion, nullifying the TD.

• In the second quarter, Washington ran a play toward the sideline, and as the players tumbled out-of-bounds, a Dallas Cowboys cheerleader was trampled and had to be hauled away on a stretcher. A hush fell over the crowd, and many fans uttered a silent prayer that the girl hadn't suffered a career-threatening breast injury.

Eventually, the Redskins would revert to the form that would drive their coach, Steve Spurrier, out of the league at the end of the year. Even after their hara-kiri act, the Cowboys led at the half, 7–6. Both teams left the field, with the exception of lineman Larry Allen. On this sultry afternoon in a stadium that seemed void of oxygen, Allen stood near the Dallas sideline, doubled over and surrounded by trainers. This did not appear to be a knee or ankle problem. Big number 73 looked like he'd just suffered a heart attack. Finally, he was evacuated. Allen was gassed.

Dallas somehow won this football game. The Tuna's assessment? He looked at the Cowboys' record, now 6–2, and said, "We're flying on a burning plane."

With the season half over and the Buffalo Bills arriving at Texas Stadium, a question was gripping the Dallas–Fort Worth area. Where in the hell was Jerry Jones? The most ubiquitous owner in the National Football League was no longer gleaming in front of the footlights. The man had disappeared from the public. With the NBA season beginning to crank up, bringing

Dallas Mavericks owner Mark "Look at me! Look at me! I'm a billionaire! Look at how cute I am! Aren't I adorable?!" Cuban back to the forefront, area sports nuts were truly starting to miss Jerry Jones.

What had happened was that the new and improved Jerry Jones was indeed doing what any and all had deemed impossible. He was allowing Bill Parcells to run his football team. Jones had other work to do. While business analysts estimated that the franchise that Jones purchased in 1989 for $140 million had increased in value six times over, Jones, like Oliver Twist with his porridge bowl, wanted some more.

Dallas Cowboys Park was his ultimate dream, which would enable him to get his "more," and Jerry was all too busy hawking the venture. The park was to consist of the following pieces.

- Dallas Cowboys Stadium. "As the anchor of Dallas Cowboys Park, the stadium will seat 75,000 fans in an air-conditioned state-of-the-art facility with a retractable roof and will feature unique, open end zones that could seat thousands more."
- Legends Square. "As the center-point of Dallas Cowboys Park, the square will serve as a must-see destination for tourists, featuring retail dining and family entertainment."
- Cowboys Field House. "This one-of-a-kind recreation center for families will feature an interactive Cowboys Hall of Fame, indoor sports action like rock climbing and, potentially, a fitness center manned by Dallas Cowboys trainers." Promotional material for Jerry's dream town further includes Cowboys Place, which is a residential and office layout, Cowboys Hotel, and Cowboys Fields, which is where kids can play soccer. *Hell,*

and that ain't all, folks. We've got the Cowboys Geisha Spa, a massage parlor where little gals imported from the Far East will let you name your pleasure. Our motto is "The Customer Comes First." And saving the best for last, wait'll you see Cowboys Exotic Nights, featuring a free buffet, where our off-duty cheerleaders not only provide the basic lap dance but throw in a couple of Franklins, and they strap a Michael Irvin Special on you!

So while the Cowboys were winning games nobody deemed possible, Jones was actively marketing his dream. Meanwhile, the city of Dallas and various suburban locations like Irving and Arlington continued to weigh the economic potential against the drawbacks—same as they would if somebody wanted to build a new prison or nuclear plant inside their city limits.

The Tuna was preparing his team for the Bills and his former bus driver from New England, Drew Bledsoe. The Bills were 4–4, living inside the playoff bubble now, and therefore lethal. The game itself followed the blueprint that Parcells and his defensive adjutant, Mike Zimmer, had drawn. Late in the first quarter, Eric Ogbogu rushed Bledsoe, relieved him of the football, and La'Roi Glover recovered it at the Bills' twenty-four. Quincy Carter turned that play into the game's only touchdown on a two-yard toss to Dan Campbell.

In the fourth quarter, with Dallas clinging to a 10–6 lead, the Bills and Bledsoe got the ball at their own twenty-four with 3:54 to play. With a heart-stopping finish looming, Buffalo fans—who'd watched their football team lose back-to-back Super Bowl games to the Cowboys and their hockey team lose a Stanley Cup Final to the Dallas Stars—naturally didn't do a damn thing. The

Bills punted, and with Parcells's ex-Jet Adrian Murrell running the ball instead of Troy Hambrick, the Cowboys kept possession for the remaining 2:51. Now they were 7–2.

Afterward, the first question Parcells faced concerned Murrell: "Is he your featured back now?"

The Tuna, momentarily, wigged out. "You guys are unbelievable," Parcells snapped at the reporter. "Just because I play somebody for a period of time, you're asking me if I flip around my lineup! I am going to play the guys who make this a successful football team. Troy Hambrick is the starting running back."

The name Bill Belichick would come up a time or two as the Cowboys launched preparations for their trip to New England to play the Patriots. Dallas, at 7–2, was still a game ahead of the Eagles in the NFC East. But naturally the talk centered on the Patriots coach and Parcells's lingering spat with his ex-comrade who the Tuna was convinced had stiffed old man Leon Hess back with the Jets. Pocketed that cool mil bonus to stick around and be the head guy and then split.

"I've got a history with just about every team we play, and everybody keeps harping on it, week in, week out," Parcells griped. "It started back with the Giants game. Hell, nobody on that team, no players or coaches, was still around from when I was there. I actually know one guy on their team, Michael Strahan, and I met him for about ten minutes at some social occasion. Same with the Jets the next week and Bledsoe last week." The Tuna stopped just short of yelling, "What the fuck do you want me to say, that I know for sure that Belichick once traded his grandmother for a thirty-five-horsepower Evinrude outboard motor?"

No, Parcells didn't quite go that far. He had nothing at all to say about Bill Belichick. The game itself, and whatever might have been left of the so-called feud between the old coaches, would live up to the nonhype that Parcells had afforded it. The Sunday night game on ESPN would attract the second-highest rating ever for a cable TV program, and it was a wall-to-wall, brain-numbing yawner. From the Cowboys' standpoint, the trip to Gillette Stadium served as a clone of the flop down at Tampa. Final: Pats 12, Cowboys 0. Back-to-back shutouts on the road. Quincy Carter threw three picks. Yet another dog's lunch.

In the Dallas–Fort Worth TV market, the New England mess provided one out-of-the-ordinary feature. On a postgame program on Dallas's Channel 8 that aired from the Cowboys locker room, a player interview was conducted while another player, in the background, appeared on camera, fresh out of the shower. The player (nobody saw his face) provided the kind of full frontal display that intrigues the hardworking female sportswriters. This guy's wasn't very long, but it was as big around as a coffee can.

Tom Landry and Bill Parcells would share at least one trait. Any fiery pregame, win-for-the-Gipper speeches were not in their repertoire.

Oh, ex-Cowboys can remember Landry getting a little emotional before some big game and addressing the squad. "There is one professional football player on this team, and that's Bob

Lilly," Landry said. "The rest of you are amateurs drawing pay. Now. Let's go get 'em."

Parcells's aversion to locker-room rhetoric as game time approaches is based on two of his basic leadership principles. The first one is that no matter what the circumstances, when addressing the workforce, keep your speech as short as possible, and better yet, don't make one at all. "The way to inspire a team is to have them well prepared at the kickoff after a good week of practice and provide them with the confidence that comes from that" is the Tuna's basic management theory.

The Carolina Panthers, at 7–2 and definitely for real, were lined up on the other side of Texas Stadium. This was yet another of those crossroads games for Parcells's team. The teams exchanged hooks and jabs, and well into the third quarter, the score was 17–17. Dallas had the ball at the Carolina sixteen-yard line. The situation was third-and-one, the same third-and-one that had proven so disgustingly futile back in Tampa Bay, and the Panthers' defense was every bit as threatening as the Bucs' in short-yardage situations.

In practice back in September, offensive coordinator Maurice Carthon had devised a play in which the fullback would take the ball, run toward left tackle, and then lateral the ball to the trailing halfback. Parcells remembered something like that from his days as a college assistant at Florida State. "The head coach down there in those days was a guy named Bill Peterson, a real eccentric." (Was he ever. On his TV show once, prior to a game against Auburn and its star runner, Tucker Fredrickson, Peterson told a live audience, "If we're gonna win this game, we've got to stop that Fucker Tedrickson.") What Parcells said that he had learned from Peterson was that if you've got something new, you'll never know if it works unless you give it a try.

So now, Parcells figured, was the right time to take the play that Carthon had devised two months earlier and, with the game on the line, give it a try. Quincy Carter brightened when the play came in and said to the team, "All right, touchdown." He handed the ball to Richie Anderson. Just as Anderson was being buried in the Dallas backfield by Carolina end Mike Rucker, he pitched the ball to Aveion Cason, who followed Flozell Adams's downfield block, cut back, and scored. Dallas won, 24–20.

Were those tears in Parcells's eyes after the game? With his sure-enough faltering, the Tuna said, "No, can't call us losers anymore. We're . . . something else now." The moment, emotional as it was, didn't last long. "By six o'clock," Parcells pointed out, "I'll guarantee you that I'll all but have forgotten this game. I'll be back at my desk, watching film and wondering how we won the game."

CHAPTER 15

THE VALLEY RANCH PENITENTIARY

NO HOSTAGES WILL EXIT THROUGH THIS GATE.

That helpful reminder is posted on the inside portions of the front and back doors at every facility in the vast network of the Texas prison system. That's a policy that prison officials put in place in 1974, when some inmates attempted to march out of the Walls Unit in Huntsville, the one where the executions happen in Texas's world-famed equal-opportunity death house, using workers from the prison library as a human shield. The law boys blew them all away, thus establishing an operational mandate geared toward eliminating the kidnapping of noncons as an exit strategy.

Bill Parcells would appreciate that. You've got to establish a set of firm rules, or the next thing you know, you've got chaos on your team. I learned about the prison signs about eight years ago, when I wrote one of those life-as-seen-from-inside-the-bars features for a magazine. One inmate, a guy named Chico, sized up the day-to-day aspect of Texas prison life. "It's just like any other place. Boys will be boys," Chico said, "and unless you can fight off three sumbitches like me at the same time, boys will be girls."

The food isn't so good either. For a while, the convicts were served a concoction known as Vita Pro. "It was like that dog chow stuff, only much worse," Chico said. "I read the ingredients they put in that shit . . . like rocket fuel. Silicon dioxide. What the hell's that? Finally, when I got a lump under my arm, I quit eating the stuff. Actually starved, but the lump went away. Then I ate some more and got this big lump on my ass. Everybody had the same problem. Dudes knottin' up all over the place."

Chico looks like a twenty-something American male who might be playing linebacker for the Bears, or somebody, except for his juvenile enthusiasms. "I went from stealing bubble gum to jacking jewelry stores," he explained. Chico detailed the recreation hour, and his eyes began to glitter like Las Vegas at Christmas season. "Lots of fights. I guess it comes natural to me. Two shots to the temple and a chop to the neck. Then, when I get them on the floor, I put the boots to 'em. That's all there is to it. Lotsa times, you don't need an excuse. Houston versus Dallas. Choose up sides, and get it on. Guerilla warfare, plain and simple."

So how does that differ from the routine experienced by players under contract for the Dallas Cowboys, or any of the other National Football League inmates? Not much, not very much at all. The significant one is that prison, as one person in a white uniform put it, "is easy to get in but hard to get out." In the NFL, it's the other way around.

Visitors to the NFL's Valley Ranch unit will see that the facilities at the football plant and the Big House are stunningly similar. The security is ironclad and the only thing that's missing at Valley Ranch is the razor wire. Back where the players dress, memorandums from the "authorities" occupy every vacant wall space.

NOTICE TO NFL PERSONNEL—Serious penalties will result from: (1) Accepting a bribe or agreeing to throw or fix a game or to illegally influence its outcome; (2) Failure to promptly report any incident in which NFL personnel have been contacted that involve such activities; (3) Betting on an NFL game; (4) Associating with gamblers or gambling activities in a manner tending to bring discredit to the game. Any noncompliance will result in fines and/or suspension from the NFL for life.

Then there's a reminder about the fines and/or eventual suspension for the utilization of the football helmet as a weapon. That's the one on which somebody pasted Darren Woodson's mug shot, as a joke. Here, players are informed how much the league tends to frown on "illegal helmet hits against defenseless players," and how it embraces a we-are-not-amused attitude regarding helmet-to-chin, helmet-to-face, and helmet-to-helmet contact, or helmet contact with a player on the ground that is also known as "spearing."

Also, the league is down on any off-the-field activities involving conduct "that endangers" the poor bastard on the street and "any crime that involves the use or threat of physical violence, including hate crimes." And here I paraphrase: If any of you motherfuckers have a problem with that, call Mike Haynes at this 800 number at the league office, and he'll be happy to explain things further. And, oh man, you ought to see the posted memo that details the league's drug policy. It's longer than a whore's dream.

No, life inside the walls of Valley Ranch is not as austere as a Texas prison. Not quite. The food on the buffet table outside the locker room, which is the coaches' noontime meal, is better. But can life be any easier under the dictatorial thumb of Warden Parcells? No, and it was about to get worse, because after the Carolina win, the Tuna confirmed that "it will be hard to keep us out of the tournament now." The tournament. That's what Parcells insists on calling the NFL playoffs. As the tournament approaches, under Bill Parcells, that's when the players learn a whole new meaning for the word "hell."

A former lineman for Parcells at New England, Bob Kratch, summed up what was in store for these Cinderella Cowboys. "He can just be brutal," Kratch said of his former boss. "But the thing is, it's usually a psyche test. He feels that if you can handle his wrath, then comes a playoff game, and he knows you can handle that situation, too."

Dallas's players milled around the locker room. After the big game against the Panthers, they would have only two actual practice days to get ready for the Dolphins and the Thanksgiving game that the Cowboys traditionally have played at home since 1966. They knew that the sessions about to begin on the field outside would be, at the mildest, intense. Matt Lehr, the Cowboys center, looked pensive, sitting in front of his locker and meticulously applying white adhesive tape around each of his fingers. "Parcells—what's kind of eerie about him is the way that he knows every damn thing that there is to know about you,"

Lehr said. "Even more than you know about yourself. He knows where your parents went to college—went to high school even, and what their high school mascots were."

If Parcells had been brutal to his football players in their abbreviated week of preparation for Miami, that was nothing compared with how brutal his team looked on Thanksgiving. After eleven regular-season games, they would implode in the twelfth. The Dolphins took the opening kickoff and started handing the ball to Ricky Williams, the former Texas Longhorn who had become the first man to win the Heisman Trophy wearing a Rastafarian hairstyle. Williams breezed down the field like he was on Rollerblades in the park. Miami never needed to run a third-down play on that opening march, and after they scored the touchdown, Derek Ross fumbled away the next kickoff. Williams fumbled it right back, but that wouldn't matter. This was a Thursday on which the Cowboys would be easy meat. They'd left their A-game back on the field against Carolina the previous Sunday.

Norv Turner, Miami's offensive coordinator who used to have the job in Dallas, was enjoying the time of his life. Whenever the Dolphins needed big yards, he would simply call for quarterback Jay Fiedler to throw a deep ball to Chris Chambers, working one-on-one against Mario Edwards. Whenever Chambers did not make the catch, Edwards would be flagged for interference. In the end, Chambers would catch five balls for ninety-six yards and three TDs. After the Dolphins had won, 40–21 (Dallas would make the final score late in the game which created the artificial impression that this might have been a contest at some point), the stat sheet showed that Miami had generated 365 net yards. It had seemed like twice that.

While his players, each chagrined, trudged through the tunnel and into the locker room, Parcells marched into the interview room to offer his impressions of the afternoon's events. After that opening loss to Atlanta, Parcells had seemed unfazed, rather cheerful. After the great win over Carolina, he was teary-eyed. Now, as darkness enshrouded North Texas on a holiday, the Tuna was pissed off. He spoke in short, sharply punctuated sentences. "We had no chance to win today," he began. "It was very poor. This team does not have the maturity for this kind of situation. We have young, distracted players who don't understand what the NFL is all about, and I can tell.

"We still have an opportunity to do something in the final month of the season. But if we continue to play like we did today, the opportunity won't make a hell of a lot of difference. So we took our beating. The only good thing about this game is that it's only one game, and we can only lose it once. But frankly, to go out and play like that on Thanksgiving on national television, I'm a little embarrassed. The players ought to be embarrassed, too, and I told them that."

Two days later, Derek Ross, the player who fumbled the kickoff after the Dolphins had scored so easily on their first drive, failed to appear for a scheduled visit to a Dallas children's hospital. During his rookie season, Ross, a cornerback from Ohio State and a third-round draft pick, had shown a gift for the NFL game and was one of the few bright spots in the smoking remains of the 2002 campaign. He had made what an NFL analyst, whatever that is, called a "dramatic impact" on the Dallas defense. Ross, who wears his hair combed in a straight-up fashion that gives him the look of a man who has just been electrocuted, led the league's rookie cornerbacks with five interceptions. His reputation was that of "a little bit of a knucklehead, with underlying good common sense."

During training camp in San Antonio, Parcells admitted that the Cowboys' secondary, one of several notable areas of vulnerability in 2002, might make a quick switch to become a "strong point" in 2003, and he mentioned Ross as a working piece in that improvement process. The night before the Cowboys' preseason game at Pittsburgh, one of my "sources" mentioned that Derek Ross had missed the team curfew but played in the game anyway. Then Ross injured a knee, had it scoped, and missed the early part of the regular season. Parcells had been on his ass, but good, after his return.

The Tuna complained that Ross wasn't aggressive enough and seemed to be babying the sore knee. But finally, Parcells had put Ross back into game action as the team's third-down nickel back. With Ross on the field, the opposing offense's third-down efficiency numbers had been steadily dropping, and then Parcells had entrusted him with running back kickoffs. He'd taken one all the way back, remember, against the Redskins, although his hundred-yard TD had been wiped out on a penalty.

As the team went back to work on Monday after the Thanksgiving fiasco to prepare for the next game, a trip to Philadelphia that would determine the winner of the NFC East, a man from Bill Parcells's personnel staff confronted Derek Ross as he stepped out of his car.

"You're not going inside, Derek," the Tuna's guy said. "You've been released."

Parcells's four-word message to the team was plain. "I'm not fucking around."

★   ★   ★

CBS, the network that carried the Dallas-Miami Thanksgiving game, conducted an interview with Quincy Carter three days before the game. The quarterback talked about his coach. "He's the closest thing to God you'll ever meet," Carter had said. "Everything that he says will happen does happen, just the way he says it will."

Back in October when the Cowboys were assembling their five-game streak, Parcells had reminded his team, and its once-again adoring fans along with it, "that you'd better buy an umbrella, because someday soon, it's going to rain. As for Quincy Carter, the time will come this year when he's going to look not-so-good and we'll get beat about forty-one to ten. How Quincy responds to that is when we'll start getting an idea of what kind of quarterback he is."

Finally, at long last, Tuna the oracle would blow one. God erred. He was flat, dead wrong. Dallas wouldn't get beat 41–10. They'd only lose 36–10. They'd picked a critical time to sustain the loss, though. Thanks to Rush Limbaugh, the Eagles and Donovan McNabb, if nothing else, had bonded. Since their game in Dallas, Philly had won six straight.

For the rematch, Andy Reid had devoted countless hours to reviewing the tapes. From that he had devised a master game plan: Don't attempt any onside kicks. Had Dallas won, the Cowboys would have been tied for the lead in the NFC East, holding the tiebreaker advantage over Philly, since Dallas would have won both meetings between the teams.

The Cowboys, though, for their third-straight road game,

were dead by the middle of the third quarter. The division title, with its bye week and probable home-field advantage for at least one playoff (uh, excuse me, Tuna, I meant to say tournament) game, was statistically distantly remote and realistically beyond hope. Now the team could only focus on making the playoffs, period. As Parcells fought to sustain the survival of this bleeding aneurysm of a football team, he had one and only one asset that he could count upon. The schedule.

In his second season, Steve Spurrier's Washington Redskins had cured more cripples than Oral Roberts. If the opposing team was suffering from anything ranging from clogged bowels to crabs, all Spurrier had to do was place both hands upon the shoulders of the afflicted and demand, "Heal! Heal!"

How truly odd that Spurrier would fail so astoundingly in the NFL. At Florida, where he'd made a habit of ridiculing the Southeast Conference archrivals he'd been beating each and every year—like Tennessee ("you can't spell Citrus [the bowl game for also-rans] without T-U") and Georgia (he'd refer to Bulldogs coach Ray Goff as Ray Goof)—Spurrier reigned as king of the imperially cocky "sun visor" coaches. Jon Gruden and his former assistant, Bob Stoops, now riding the showboat at Oklahoma, had copied Spurrier's sideline look.

Washington owner Daniel Snyder, in his zeal to win, hadn't given Spurrier a fat contract. No, Snyder gave Spurrier a tanker full of green ink and told him to go and print his own money. Even Bill Parcells, when he was still clinging to the public notion that he would never return to pro coaching, had joked that he might reconsider "if somebody would pay me $1 million a year more than Steve Spurrier's getting."

So, in what would be Spurrier's next-to-last game as the Redskins' coach, Dallas flew to Washington and got well. With Patrick Ramsey hurt, the 'Skins were using Tim Hasselbeck as quarterback. Tim used to be a ball boy in practices when Parcells was coaching the Giants. Hasselbeck, if nothing else, will be remembered for placing Dallas rookie cornerback Terrence Newman, the first-round pick, on the fast track to becoming an all-pro. Newman got three interceptions against the 'Skins, tying a Dallas team record. The Cowboys won, 27–0, after allowing Washington 161 total yards—a number that Spurrier would have expected after his first two possessions back when he was at Florida.

A week later, another entry on the league's intensive care list and another coach on his way out—the Giants and Jim Fassel—came to Texas Stadium and made life easy as the Cowboys scored early. New York never fired a shot, and Dallas won, 19–3. That sealed the deal. Dallas was in the playoffs, and Parcells's only problem was to continue to insist that this wasn't his best single season of coaching a football team. No, that had happened in 1999, when his 1–5 Jets had managed to finish 8–8. Since most Dallas fans had never really *heard* of the New York Jets, they didn't believe the Tuna.

Thanks to Parcells, it was once again stylish to wear their Cowboys jerseys to church. Now, though, the number 8 with "Aikman" stitched across the back had been replaced by number 31 and "Williams," for the guy who was now the symbol of

Dallas's new search-and-destroy defense that, statistically, was the best in the National Football League.

Dallas had one regular-season game left, at New Orleans. The game didn't mean anything. Dallas, as wild card, would travel throughout the tournament. The opening game might be at Green Bay. It might be at St. Louis. It might be at Minnesota or at Carolina. Each one was a bad bargain. So what? Looking back, Dallas probably would have had a better chance of landing in those 2012 Olympic games than landing in the 2003 NFL playoffs.

The mood in the Cowboys' dressing room in preparation for the Saints was business as usual. For all that the players knew, Parcells was watching them on some hidden surveillance device, making sure that nobody was laughing, playing grab ass, or thinking about anything but football.

Back during the less disciplined times that began during the slap-happy coaching regime of Barry Switzer, the middle of the room was occupied by a Ping-Pong table and a card table upon which Emmitt Smith presided over the domino competitions. Those domino games often seemed more bitterly contested than the football games on Sunday. The game-room effect is no longer in place in there, and the table in the locker room now contains a big stack of footballs that the players are supposed to autograph before the balls are donated to various charities.

La'Roi Glover sat in front of his locker looking somber. I asked him, the only player on this team who could meet the Tuna's how-to-talk-to-the-media protocols and still have something to say, if he could define the formula that Parcells had utilized to magically transform this assembly of previous nothingness into the playoffs.

"A formula?" said Glover. "Yeah, there's a formula, and it's really very simple. He kicks your ass ninety-five percent of the time and pats your ass the other five percent. Parcells is everything he's advertised to be. He doesn't take any crap, he doesn't hide anything, and he holds everybody accountable."

Glover was one of four Cowboys players who had been placed on the NFC Pro Bowl roster. "After the Pro Bowl list came out, he congratulated the four of us who were on it, in front of the team, before practice," Glover said. "And then, in practice, he climbed all over our butts. In fact, he spread it on pretty thick. I let some back run past me on a draw play. I can hear him now. 'What the fuck's the matter with you, Glover? What the fuck is fuckin' with you?' Then, I let my arms kind of windmill when I was trying to get off a block and rush the passer, and here he came again. 'All you're fuckin' doing is swimming! You trying to make the Olympics?'

"Then, finally, I was showing some rookie guy something that might improve his technique, and Parcells comes strolling over. 'La'Roi, your grandfather was a coach. Your father, too. And somebody said you might want to be one, too, right?' I said, 'Yeah, coach, that's right.' And he yells, 'Well, they've got an assistant's opening over at SMU! If you want to fuckin' coach, why don't you just get your fuckin' ass over there!'"

Glover grinned and repeated his Tuna impersonation. "They've got a fuckin' opening at SMU!" Then he threw his head back and laughed out loud.

Dallas got beat at New Orleans, 13–7. Troy Hambrick needed to gain sixty-six yards against the Saints to accomplish a one-thousand-yard rushing season. He would gain only twenty-six. Carter threw three interceptions. Parcells didn't care. His only genuine disappointment in the loss was that it leveled Dallas's road record for the regular season at 4–4. A winning record on the road is one of the prime keystones that the Tuna uses to gauge a successful season. Since jumping off that 5–1 start, the Cowboys had been riding what Parcells termed a seesaw for the remainder of the season, and he cited the team's immaturity as the reason. The tournament was beginning and Dallas was in it. "Now, we are here," the Tuna said. "Now we're getting to see what's what."

The Cowboys were playing at Carolina Saturday night. They had beaten the Panthers already. Why not again? If Parcells's one-man jury was still out on certain members of the squad, the playoffs would remove most doubts. "These games are too much for certain players," he conceded. As far as using playoff performance as the most telling measuring device, Parcells did point out that "unless you win the Super Bowl, the last thing you remember isn't that good."

Thursday, which happened to be New Year's Day 2004, would be the Cowboys' final day for serious practice before leaving for Carolina the following afternoon. I decided to make the drive out to Valley Ranch in hopes that, since this was a holiday and all, the media throng might be thinned out.

I walked into the locker room. The media not only had thinned out, there was nobody in there. Nobody except me and Larry Allen, who was slowly putting on his body armor. That's when it sank in. Media time in the locker room was over. I wasn't supposed to be in there. "Oh, well. Too late now. Let's try to talk to Larry."

From midseason on, Larry Allen had not reverted to his

greatest-in-the-history-of-the-NFL form, but he and his aching body and Bill Parcells, after a war of wills, had evidently reached some sort of compromise. Allen had played, played hard, and played well on certain occasions. He'd been named to the NFC Pro Bowl squad. Granted, that bouquet was largely due to Allen's reputation, his years of distinguished service in the league. No matter the reputation, a guy must at least show up and be somebody in order to get the all-expenses-paid trip to Hawaii, and Allen had at least done that.

Now I was introducing myself and thinking, Goddamn, this guy is big. Seriously, up close, Larry Allen is the size of a pecan tree. I could take most of my personal belongings and live comfortably inside either one of his legs. Allen's reputation is that he is a man of few words, usually, and otherwise no words at all. His responses to a few generic questions ranged from five to seven words.

Finally, I said, "Do you get along with Bill Parcells?"

Larry Allen said nothing. He just stared at me in utter disbelief, but it was a look that spoke eloquently, a look that said, "You dumb fuck, if you only knew . . ." Then Allen actually smiled, shook his head, and walked out of the locker room and onto the practice field where he knew that Bill Parcells, the antagonist of his lifetime, would be waiting for him.

CHAPTER 16

TO THE LAND OF GOODY'S HEADACHE POWDER

Bumper stickers that read "Thank You for Smoking" can be located on cars traveling along the Billy Graham Expressway in Charlotte. The smoke pouring from beneath the hoods of the vehicles bearing the bumper stickers indicates that the cars have a five-pack-a-day habit themselves.

Other than the frequently articulated local sentiment that the surgeon general can go fuck himself—what does he know?—the Carolina gentry maintain a charm and gentleness, and they use Mountain Dew as the prime ingredient in the best damn Jell-O salad you'll ever eat. You can also purchase Goody's Headache Powder in certain precincts of the Carolinas, and if you've never tried this stuff, you're missing something. It'll set you free. If they sold that stuff in Dallas, Michael Irvin would never have appeared in any courtrooms.

These lovely Carolinas remain chin-deep in sports tradition. No place on this continent, and therefore no place on earth, contains a populace so ardent, so passionate when it comes to certain categories of the sporting life. God, the memories. Talk about hoop dreams. What school has ever provided fans with a more joyous memory than that of Duke's Christian Laettner hitting that half-court buzzer-beater that KO'd Kentucky in the greatest Sweet Sixteen finals ever played, back in 1992? Well, the Tarheels can, and have on various occasions, such as the time in 1957 when they beat Kansas and Wilt Chamberlain in the triple-overtime that some people call the most thrilling NCAA Final Four game ever played. How do you top that? The late Jim Valvano, the immortal Jimmy V. up there in hoops heaven, he can tell you. That basket that enabled the North Carolina State Wolfpack to beat Houston's Phi-Slamma-Jamma lingers as real today as it was in 1983.

Of course, when you get off a plane and walk through the lobby of the Charlotte airport, those life-size cardboard figures you see everywhere aren't ACC basketball icons. Not unless basketball players have taken to wearing flame-retardant jumpsuits that advertise DeWalt tools, Miller Lite, or Home Depot.

Remember, when you're in Carolina, you're as deep in the heart of NASCAR as a human being can get. After Dale Earnhardt died at Daytona in 2001, every commercial building in the entire region—every liquor store, gas station, and mom-and-pop grocery—was decorated like a Buddhist shrine in honor of the memory of the late Intimidator, Driver Number Three, God rest his soul. The fact that a freeway is named after Billy Graham naturally indicates that these people are deep in the faith, and that's what got them through the grief process.

They had to be so proud of Dale, Jr., the Little E, when he returned to that Daytona track not five months after his daddy had died to win the Fourth of July Pepsi Firecracker 400. Before the race, the TV interviewer asked Junior about his heavy heart, and he said, "Aw, hell. I got over that a long time ago."

The Carolina people don't just get off on college basketball and stock-car racing, either. They're big on bowling and bass fishing and minor-league baseball, as evidenced in *Bull Durham,* but when it comes to football, that's where they get off the bus. Name the greatest moment in North Carolina gridiron history. Not just *the* greatest—name *any* great event. Betcha can't. Lawrence Taylor played collegiately at Chapel Hill, but he had to go to New York before the Tuna could transform LT into a national celebrity.

Now if you want to dig into the deepest mists of football trivia, you'll find that the 1942 Rose Bowl game was played in North Carolina. Yep. That happened because the Duke Blue Devils managed to field a good team that season, good enough to get invited to the Rose Bowl. In the weeks after Pearl Harbor, everybody was jittery in California and fearful that a big assembly of people in Pasadena might tempt the Japs to pull some shit. So they moved the game to Durham.

So when the Cowboys came to Ericsson Stadium (seems like they should rename the place after the Intimidator instead of some damn Swede who's over here trying to peddle cell phones), this might have been the biggest frenzy over a football game in North Carolina since, well, the 1942 Rose Bowl game. The place was jammed with 73,014 fans. Parcells had predicted that his players would sense they were entering a different and more challenging environment now that this was a playoff game—and a night playoff game at that. What's different about a night game? Well, the fans have five or so extra hours to get snot-slinging drunk, that's what.

Parcells stood on the sidelines as kickoff time approached. He was wearing a jacket with a small *D* emblazoned on it. The thing looked like a high school letter jacket from back in the 1940s. All it needed was a little football-shaped patch on the right sleeve, with "city champs" stitched on it. The Tuna knew what might happen if Dallas could win here—the road win in the playoffs is what touches off those impossible dreams that manly baritones sing about on Broadway. Parcells had seen it work with his 1984 Giants. They'd gone to L.A. and beaten the Rams in the opening round of the playoffs, back when the "tournament" that led to the Super Bowl was only a two-week affair. His Giants stayed on the coast all week and wound up losing at San Francisco to a team that Parcells regards as the best of the championship teams that the 49ers fielded in that era. "But we beat the 49ers in the playoffs the next year and won the Super Bowl the year after that," he liked to remind people. Maybe Dallas would emulate the formula. Then again . . .

Soon after the game started, it seemed that Carolina coach John Fox might have watched *60 Minutes* within the previous month, when Lawrence Taylor was featured on a segment. Taylor owned up to something that had been his favorite pregame tactic during his playing days. LT said that he would dispatch some, well, friendly working girls up to the hotel room of the opposing team's star players the night before certain big games. Keep 'em up all night, and they won't give any 110 percent the next day.

Casey Stengel used to say this about the nocturnal habits of his baseball players. "It don't bother me that one of my players might be up all night with a woman," Casey declared. "What bothers me is a player who's up all night *looking* for a woman." Yeah, Casey, but what about this modern genre of professional athlete, when they're up all night with *three* women.

This is not to imply that John Fox had managed to smuggle any professional hostesses into the rooms of Dallas football players prior to the playoff game. Given the airtight, maximum security scrutiny that Parcells imposes upon his troops when they travel, any visitors would have to gain entry to the hotel rooms via the air-conditioning ducts. (Although, having seen Irvin's party friends firsthand, they were small enough to have wiggled through.)

After Dallas punted on its first possession, Panthers quarter-back Jake Delhomme threw a pass to Steve Smith, and Smith ran down the field for seventy yards before being apprehended. Dallas held the Panthers to a field goal, but it was already evident that the Dallas miracle season was about to deflate. Did it ever. The Panthers won going away, 29–10. The fact that Carolina would go on the road to St. Louis, and then to Philadelphia, and keep on winning until Adam Vinatieri beat them in the dying seconds of the Super Bowl, that wouldn't offer any pain relief for the Cowboys' meager effort in Charlotte.

This loss, ugly as it was, couldn't be labeled as one of those team efforts, though. The usually reliable running back, one of the Tuna's favorite guys, was responsible for two major botches in the first half that allowed the game to get out of control. Richie Anderson dropped a screen pass with nothing but open field awaiting him downfield. "He probably didn't see the ball coming," said Parcells, giving an alibi for his guy afterward. "That was a touchdown, it looked like to me. That was going to be a big, big play."

With Dallas approaching the Carolina end zone in the second

quarter, Anderson fumbled away the ball, and the game, near the Panthers' ten-yard line. "It just slipped out" was all that Anderson could say.

Of course, there might be some blood on the hands of the Tuna here, too. Not from the fact that he'd signed Anderson, his former Jet, as a teacher's pet. The previous spring, Delhomme, the Panthers' quarterback who'd thrown for 273 yards in routing the Cowboys, had come through Valley Ranch on a tryout, and Parcells had passed. He figured that Delhomme, being a Louisiana Cajun, would probably get his foot bitten off by an alligator during the off-season, and the Tuna couldn't afford to take the chance. He probably regretted that now.

The Tuna's postgame demeanor after the Carolina collapse offered all of the good cheer and optimism of act 3 in *Death of a Salesman*. His face reflected nothing but vanished hope and wistful despair. So the casual onlooker was thinking, What an act. The guy is overjoyed just to be standing here. And he's relieved that it ended here because 29–10 looks almost respectable compared to the ass-kicking this team would have received had it advanced deeper into the playoffs. The casual onlooker is also flat, dead wrong. The locusts were chewing up the Tuna's insides just as they always do when his team gets beaten, and the depth of the torment becomes even worse after it happens in a playoff. Remember what Parcells said regarding his aversion to lounge acts. Now he'd just bombed in the big room. Some reporter started to press Parcells about his team's offensive performance against the Panthers. What could he say? His quarterback hadn't done much of a job quarterbacking, and his running backs sure as hell hadn't run. The camera doesn't lie.

"Obviously," Parcells said, "there will be changes."

EPILOGUE

The media were back, for the last time, at Valley Ranch to hear Bill Parcells's State of the Team address. Three days had passed since the team's unfortunate closing chapter back there in the smoky foothills of Appalachia, where the roaring engine of Dale Earnhardt's Mr. Goodwrench Chevy racecar echoes to this day.

Three days were enough for Parcells, wearing blue sweats, to appear rested, almost at peace, although the interim had not been uneventful. His defensive coordinator, Mike Zimmer, had visited Lincoln, Nebraska, and received an offer to become head coach of the Cornhuskers. So Parcells, with the approval of Jerry Jones, had fashioned a counteroffer that Zimmer could not refuse. Now, the same thing was happening with Sean Payton—the offensive assistant. Al Davis was about to dangle the head-coaching position of the Oakland Raiders under Payton's nose the following day. And guess what? Payton would decline as well.

Parcells was talking about the past season and what was going to happen next. If there had been any lingering doubt that Parcells had just completed his best work as a pro football coach—and he continued to insist that had happened with the 1999 Jets—nobody could deny that Jerry Jones, the owner, had accomplished his best job ever of owning. He'd hired Parcells and, contrary to everybody's prediction, had remained not only hidden backstage but practically invisible the entire year.

With every media outlet in the entire market triple-teaming the end-of-the-year press conference, an event shrouded in glad tidings, Jones again was nowhere on the premises. Was it possible that Arkansas's ultimate gift to the Lone Star State had declared himself *persona non grata* in his own damn football complex? A more reasonable suggestion might be that Jones was extracting huge measures of devilish delight in confounding his critics, the ones who had been so persistent in their insistence that the Cowboys were a doomed franchise because Jerry Jones was one kid you'd never keep out of the candy store. Jones, now seemingly immersed in the newly discovered joys of an off-camera life, had become an overnight testimonial to the principles of self-restraint. Jones's Dallas counterparts, namely Mark Cuban, the Richard Simmons of NBA owners, and Tom Hicks, who maintains a heliport at the front door of the baseball park in Arlington to keep reminding himself that he's rich, could do well to watch the New Jerry.

"What we have done is come from the bottom of the league, and now we're at the middle of the pack," was Parcells's first declaration. Then he added that while the team would be improved from a personnel standpoint in 2004, and probably significantly, that was no guarantee of an upgrade on the 10–6 record. Such were the ways of the modern NFL world. But by going the cheap route during the 2003 off-season and avoiding free-agent temptations like quarterback Brian Griese, the team now had salary-cap room for more ambitious upgrades. The problem now facing Parcells was that the team's most pressing needs—they needed a big-time running back and a big-time pass rusher and somebody to challenge Quincy Carter at quarterback—happened to be the most expensive items on the shelves of NFL free-agency retail stores. Offensive linemen were available at the Home Depot, but for what the Cowboys needed, they'd have to hit the boutiques of Rodeo Drive.

"This isn't going to be a simple, overnight, one-stop-does-all process," Parcells cautioned. "This isn't like driving into the Texaco station, where you tell the guy to change the plugs and adjust the brakes. I don't want to get us in salary-cap purgatory," Parcells said. "I won't go for one or two big-ticket items. That's how you paint yourself into a corner. We're going to be prudent. No, prudent is not the right word. We're going to be, uh, judicious." Now, how many pro football coaches know the difference in nuance of the words "prudent" and "judicious," much less give a damn?

Here, Parcells was offering a vivid display of his ongoing technique of how-to-deal-with-the-media. It's the same approach that television's ultimate father figure, Ward Cleaver, imparted upon Wally and the Beav when it came to domestic success: It's not lying to the wife if you don't tell her everything. Big Bill enthusiastically embraces that philosophy when addressing a room full of microphones. So, while the Tuna was telling the truth when he said that he'd like to stockpile more linebackers for the 2004 season, he omitted the fact that he was actively pursuing a trade that would bring Keyshawn Johnson from Tampa to Dallas in exchange for Joey Galloway and that the deal was all but done.

Regarding the quarterback issue, the Tuna said that he'd rather build around Quincy Carter than go and buy somebody to replace him. "The better the team you have, the less reliant you are on your quarterback," he pointed out.

And, while Parcells *did* confirm that Carter's backup, Chad Hutchinson, would shortly be heading off to sharpen his skills playing for the Rhine Fire in NFL-Europe, he did *not* add that the team had bought Hutchinson a one-way ticket. Nor did he add that the decision was already in place to bring in another ex–baseball player, Drew Henson, whom Cowboys scouts deemed a better potential prospect than Troy Aikman.

Parcells finally summed up Year 1 of his Texas experience. "As far as an anxiety-provoking season, it wasn't that bad, really, as I look back on it. You know how sometimes you wake up in the middle of the night, like two or three in the morning, and you're sort of overcome with this awful feeling of dread, and you throw up in your mouth? That didn't happen very much, not this year," he confided.

Parcells added that his prime off-season objective was to lose weight. Charlie Tuna had come to resemble Moby Dick.

Throw up in your mouth? Jesus. After thirty-nine years, no wonder Parcells's wife finally divorced him.

Then the Tuna actually thanked the media for what he'd regarded as a reasonably untroubled working relationship. Of course, it was the Texas media that should have been thanking Bill Parcells. He'd been the most charismatic character they'd had to write about since David Koresh.

The Tuna and his Season in the Sun, that was over. The bugles were finally silent. While the Tuna walked back to his office and the reporters filed out of the front door of Valley Ranch, something attracted me back to the locker room. It was sealed off from the media, of course, and largely empty, but from inside, I could hear voices. I had no idea who was in there talking. It might have been players, it might have been coaches, it might have been friends of Jerry Jones, like Prince Bandar or somebody. I listened, hoping perhaps to overhear something that might be symbolically appropriate to this genuinely amazing, if not inspirational, football season.

One guy was talking about a person from his past, someone from his old hometown.

"Yeah," the voice said, "I'll always remember him. They called him Crazy Bobby."

"Why'd they call him Crazy Bobby?" asked the other voice.

"Because he used to let his brother fuck him in the ass."

ACKNOWLEDGMENTS

About eight years ago, I wrote a book that described the various dysfunctions of the lovable losers who played for the Texas Rangers baseball teams in the early 1970s. In early January 2003, I concocted the notion of producing an update—charting the misadventures of a last-place team with its sulking jillionaire shortstop, Alex Rodriguez.

Fortunately, my Dallas-based literary "adviser," Jim Donovan, was hasty to point out that while the Rangers were still losers, they were no longer lovable, and that one-too-many books had already been written about that suck-ass franchise. The far better story was shortly to be enacted in the North Texas sports market with the arrival of Bill Parcells, who was heading to Texas to work for owner Jerry Jones and coach the Dallas Cowboys.

So the notion to produce this Tuna book, as well as the title, was concocted by Jim Donovan. He therefore deserves some of the credit and all of the blame for whatever the outcome. The same can be said for Mauro DiPreta, senior editor at Harper-Collins, a man of vision who somehow sensed a year in advance that the Tuna's first team in Dallas would post a 10–6 record and make the playoffs. Thanks also go to his associate, Joelle Yudin.

As far as identifying the various sources for the material contained in the Tuna book, there aren't very many. Almost everything here was obtained by me, with the exception of some

ACKNOWLEDGMENTS

information that appeared in an article in *Fortune* written by John Helyar. The rest is largely the product of standard media access to the Cowboys. Which is plenty. Stats. Quotes. Injury reports. Team history. The volume of data provided by the Dallas Cowboys' media relations staff—Rich Dalrymple, Brett Daniels, and Doug Hood—is astounding.

I did receive some assistance from a couple of individuals with a little "insider" access to the Cowboys. They have already been compensated for their help with some pretty decent bottles of red wine, so it is not necessary to mention their names here.

It is important, however, that I thank Rick Steed, purveyor of forttours.com, for his ceaseless flow of ideas and perceptions regarding life in Texas, past and present. The same applies to Bert and Leon Walters, who offered encouragement, and to the people who make Red Bull, a product that provides stamina.

Ultimately, I want to express my love and gratitude to Karen G. Shropshire, a combination of beauty and sensitivity that can only be found in a recently certified Irish citizen.